Praise for Chica

"What I love about Kara's writing in both *Chill* and *Chica* is the realness and relatability. Kara's writing hits the heart and allows you to connect to your own inner journey as you read. *Chica* makes you want to take action and live the extraordinary life each of us has within us. I highly recommend reading *Chica* and using the exercises—it will spark your soul and lift your feet to walk your path!"

Andrea Carter, CEO & Founder of Success On Fire Academy™ and Wealthy Woman Warrior™ Global Training Programs

"I love Kara Deringer. She's not one of those teachers who says one thing and lives another but someone who is honest, authentic and walks her talk. She knows the formula for creating a life you love and shares that formula in her insightful, practical, and uniquely witty Kara-way. You'll love her personal stories and easy-to-read prose in *Chica*—but most of all, you'll love how happiness and success begin to unfold for you in ways you didn't think were even possible."

Debra Poneman, Bestselling *Chicken Soup for the Soul* Author and Founder of Yes to Success Seminars

CREATING HAPPY, INSPIRING AND CURIOUS ADVENTURES

KARA DERINGER

ISBN 978-0-9947987-2-5 paperback
ISBN 978-0-9947987-3-2 eBook

For information about special discounts for bulk purchases,
please contact the publisher:

FLYING COLORS PRESS
info@flyingcolors.ca

Acknowledgments

Thank you to my readers and coaching clients. I absolutely love hearing about, and seeing, the transformation you are creating in your lives. Thank you especially to my coaching clients who trust in me and implement my teachings to create extraordinary love and success in your lives... which touches your families and the world.

I am extremely grateful for my children and partner, who continually encourage me to keep teaching and writing. They light me up with their ability to bring forward their own divine bouts of profound wisdom.

My two editors have worked diligently for hour after hour to ensure that this book lands beautifully in the hearts, minds, and souls of those who read it. You have infused this book with love. Thank you for your commitment.

With deep gratitude, I would like to thank the extraordinary women who have authentically shared their stories. The learning and growth that comes from storytelling is profound, and so I acknowledge you for your immense contributions.

For those who are mentioned in this book, thank you for being you. You are bright lights. It is my honor to have crossed paths in this life with you. Let's keep spreading light in the world together. You all move me to keep on with my mission.

 *Thank you.*

Contents

Introduction

"Life is either a great adventure or nothing."

HELEN KELLER

Fans of *Chill: Creating Happiness in Life and Love* keep talking about how they love the concept of flow, which I wrote about in the first chapter. (Go to www.karaderinger.com/books.) Many people have shared with me that they've been able to create more flow in their lives – their ability to balance taking action, with trusting in synchronicity, has been strengthened. More importantly, my coaching clients have had extraordinary success in shifting their lives to be more simple, efficient, productive, synchronistic, fulfilling, and fun. It is invigorating and rewarding for me to live out my mission and support people in creating this newfound and refreshing level of success in their lives.

So, at first, I planned to title this book *Flow: A Fun, Loving, Original Woman*. But, when I saw the draft book covers with "Flow" pasted across the top, the book just didn't look right. One evening, as my partner and I were sitting having dinner, I pulled out my phone to show him some draft cover designs. He chuckled and said, "Wow! Really?! Flow?! Like how's your flow – light or heavy? Let's talk about periods and floooooow ladies." I burst out laughing and said, "I know. It doesn`'t work."

He suggested, "How about Chica?" I pondered and said in a light and curious tone, "Hm. I like it."

He went on to say, "Yeah,... you know, now that we have learned how to 'chill', it's time for fun! Let's party chica! Fiesta!"

See, my partner is Mexican, and I have to say that I am extremely grateful that he has been teaching me about how to bring more fun and relaxation into my life, while still maintaining my busy schedule and creating my dreams. I have had so, so, so much fun in the last few years. When we are out, people actually comment to us that we truly look happy.

The art of creating happiness in life and love takes awareness, practice, and commitment – and so does the art of creating adventures. Only when we become aware of how we have been blocking extraordinary success and magic in our lives, can we make a choice to live differently. Only when we connect to our mission and passions, can we clear the void that is percolating in our bodies, minds, and souls. (This is the first critical step that I teach participants in my "Powerful Purpose and Passion" program –. www.karaderinger.com/events)

When your raison d' être is clear, every day is an adventure. Last year, I put the words "Wondrous Weekdays" onto my goal board. I didn't want to wait for the weekend to do the things that are important to me and to have fun. I wanted to spend quality time with my partner and kids, enjoy healthy and delicious meals, get exercise, attend events, make progress on my community projects, etc. on weekdays and weekends.

It has become clear to me that my gift is to empower women to look after themselves, so that they can pursue higher purposes, contributing to important causes, their communities, and global innovations. I believe that there are many women who have an inner calling, and know that they would find deep satisfaction living out a higher purpose, but they feel consumed by their day to day affairs. By connecting to intuition and creating magic, I continue to be blown away, as clients I work with unleash positive

Chica 10

energy, connect to a higher purpose, and create extraordinary results in their lives.

As always, it is an honor to share my thoughts and experiences with you, and to have the opportunity to make a difference in your life. And, it is my honor to share with you the stories of four absolutely extraordinary women, who have generously and vulnerably revealed the paths they have taken, the hurdles they have hopped over, the mountains they have climbed, and the lessons they have learned. While the "Wonderful Women's Stories" were placed at the end of *Chill*, I wanted to try something new with weaving stories through *Chica*. I wish you the very best as you journey through *Chica*.

*Let's create a world full of happy and
loving people together.*

Jump!

"A lot of people ask me, 'How did you have the courage to walk up to record labels when you were 12 or 13 and jump right into the music industry?' It's because I knew I could never feel the kind of rejection that I felt in middle school. Because in the music industry, if they're gonna say no to you, at least they're gonna be polite about it."

TAYLOR SWIFT

We are all presented with opportunities every day. Sometimes the ride slows down, sometimes it actually stops in front of us, and other times it's whizzing by. One of the keys to living a curious and adventurous life is to be courageous and creative, and to jump on board.

The thing is, the ride isn't going to stop just because you think you're not the right person, or that you're not ready. It's going to keep on moving, whether you get on board or not. The universe provides an opportunity for you to join in the adventure for a moment in time, whether it is seconds, minutes, hours, days, or weeks. But if you don't get on board, the ride will move on to pick up other people who are open and willing to jump on.

We can learn to jump. We can develop the stamina to keep jumping continuously; and we can learn to recover from our falls. We train ourselves to jump faster, higher, and longer than we ever have before, which allows us to create a life that is full of extraordinary adventures and success.

Be Willing

I think one of the keys to mastering the practice of jumping into opportunities is to be willing to be anyone. We all have a notion of who we think we are: shy, independent, nice, financially responsible, conservative, or something else. We say, "I'm not entrepreneurial like that," or "I'm not promiscuous like that," or "I'm not a leader like that." But we can be anyone we want to be if we just make that simple choice.

Now, many people say, "But Kara, why would you recommend that I be someone who I'm not? I thought you believe in integrity and living in alignment with your passions? I don't want to move away from who I am, and my path." I agree. We always need to be true to our core values such as respect, integrity, honesty, fairness, responsibility, etc. But we can still live in alignment with our core values, and push ourselves to be someone we didn't think we could be when opportunities roll along.

In one example, I was at Coco Bongo in Mexico with my partner and his dad. This is an enormous nightclub that offers shows throughout the night, with performances by impersonators of Madonna, Elvis, Michael Jackson, Spiderman, and others. The show is absolutely magnificent. There are different ticket tiers for the show: jam-packed floor level, jam packed upper balcony levels,

Chica 14

and seated tables (which require you to buy a $100+ bottle of alcohol). We were seated at a table.

Phase One: As the music pumped through the speakers, and oxygen was being pumped into the air, I had an urge to stand up and dance. It didn't look like my partner and his dad were going to dance, but the seated table dancing just wasn't going to cut it for me with the energy in the club. As I stood next to our table, I felt my body gently moving to the music in the extremely tight two-foot radius of our table area.

Phase Two: My enthusiasm to dance escalated as the minutes ticked by and as some of my favorite songs blasted. I looked to my left, one tier above us, and saw a couple seated at a table, which you'd be able to pack four people around. I asked if the couple if they would mind if I danced in the open space beside their table. They agreed, and so I hopped up. My partner began passing my drink up to me, but the more I danced, the less I wanted to drink.

Phase Three: Throughout the night, on the breaks between the impersonation performances, cameras were panning the audience and projecting hot girls in a hot mess having a hot time onto giant screens. You guessed it. At one point, I saw myself on the big screen (despite the fact that my outfit and dance moves were quite a bit more conservative than many of the other girls who had been videoed). When the camera picked me up the first time (yes, it happened more than once), I could feel a rush of anxiety, and then excitement, and then pride. Oh my goodness! For a moment, I felt like Madonna myself!

Let's just say that the dancing adventure was a breakthrough out of my comfort zone. Ten years ago, I would not have even entered the first phase of standing up to dance by our table. I would have sat contentedly at the table with my two male companions, who were happily taking in all of the scenery. In fact, I'd been to Mexico a number of times in previous years and hadn't even been up for going to Coco Bongo at all.

I push myself to stretch my comfort zone frequently. As soon as an opportunity arises, whether I am slightly curious or adamantly against the idea, I remind myself that this is an opportunity for me to prove to myself that I can be someone new – like a new flavor of myself. Often I'll then catch my internal dialogue saying, "Maybe later," or "I can't do it," or "That's just not me," and I push myself to do it anyway.

We can constantly strengthen our practice of being a new version of ourselves. We can constantly push the boundaries of who we think we are, to discover what we are actually capable of. The more I push myself to do things like dance at Coco Bongo and embrace my big screen appearance, the more I develop my courage and confidence to do other things. Striking conversation and building authentic relationships in a room filled with highly successful entrepreneurs, or speaking on stage in front of thousands of people, suddenly becomes more do-able after Coco Bongo.

We can also push ourselves little by little. For instance, at one point, my partner was strongly hinting that he wanted me to wear more eyeliner and mascara. He'd say, "Your eyes are beautiful. You should, you know, highlight them more." At first, a story played in my mind that he wanted me to be someone I'm not, and that he doesn't appreciate my natural beauty. But then one day I thought, "Oh, why the hell not," and I went out and bought a pencil.

Whether it's a new endeavor that's big or small, it's amazing the feelings and stories we let come in the way of shifting and taking risks.

I think we need to be realistic about the risks of taking a chance and jumping. One of my favorite questions to ask myself is, "Is anyone going to die?" This is a good reality check. Another question I ask myself is, "If my parents found out, would they be disappointed? And do I care?" This question helps me to test and distinguish my own values.

Have you ever watched people doing something, caught yourself being envious or disgusted, and then noticed yourself being defensive? Maybe they are riding a roller coaster, or running, or making out in a park, or partying, or eating a giant salad. There's a moment of intrigue or longing or envy or loathing – and then you quickly tell yourself that you don't actually want to do that, or need to do that. Maybe you say, "That's not something I see as fun. I'm a low-key person." Or maybe you say, "I'm okay on my own. I'm independent. I don't need someone else to make me happy." Or maybe a promotion opportunity or a business opportunity pops up, and even though your heart skips a beat about the extraordinary possibilities that could come of the opportunity, you say, "I don't have the right qualifications. And it's not the right timing anyway."

See, the intrigue, longing, envy, and loathing represent the same energy at its root. It's simply an energy of resistance, of pushing away. The intrigue and longing are deep wishes that you could embrace and experience the opportunity. The envy and loathing are deep fears that perhaps that you can't or you won't – that you don't have what it takes.

When and how do you stop yourself from jumping? What are some recent examples of opportunities (little or big) that you held back on? And who did you say you are to justify not jumping on the opportunities?

1. _____

2. _____

3. _____

4. _____

5. _____

How you justify holding back on opportunities is often a blind spot, so it's extremely helpful to have a coach explore this with you. Sometimes just by being curious and self-reflecting, you'll be able to see what you've been longing for or pushing away from, and what has been holding you back. Other times, it takes someone else to spot what you've been blind to, and to cut through the stories you've been telling yourself.

I believe in living an extraordinary life, which means having extraordinary relationships, extraordinary fun, extraordinary abundance, and an extraordinary mission, but failing to jump on opportunities in any area of life severely limits creating an extraordinary life. There is no delineation between one area of life and the next. The higher your energy and the stronger your ability to jump in one area of life, the more likely you are able to attract positivity and fulfilment in other areas of life. (Go now to www.karaderinger.com/books for your gift download. Get a jump on creating *your* extraordinary life.)

Jump Fast

When you spot an opportunity, how fast do you jump? There's something to be said for the sayings "early bird gets the worm," and "first come, first served." This doesn't mean that we trample others as we zip in for the catch. It means that we make a quick decision based on our intuition, and move swiftly and gracefully in to claim what the universe has put in front of us.

After separating from my children's dad, I lived in my mom's condo for six months waiting for construction on the townhome that I had purchased to be completed. My kids and I had been living in our new townhome for about six months when I saw an "Open House" sign one Sunday afternoon in the neighboring subdivision.

The agent's name on the sign happened to be a student who I had taught at the university, so I thought it would be fun to pay him a visit.

I followed the directional arrows to the open house, walked through the home, and chatted with my former student. I commented to him that I'd lived in the area for about eight years and am always interested in real estate. I said, "You know, I actually really like this house." I asked him for the listing information sheet.

The sheet indicated that the price had been reduced significantly. I wasn't surprised. I know from experience that a vacant property generally doesn't show well. The energy feels empty and a bit dark. I had noticed that the very few pieces of furniture and accents that had been left behind did not compliment the home well. The yard needed some TLC, likely because the owners had known for a few seasons that they would be moving into a new home, lessening their commitment to the yard's upkeep.

The next day, I was still thinking about the home, so I texted my girlfriend who is a real estate agent. I mentioned the property, and said that I had walked through it, liked the layout and finishings, and thought it may be a good deal. She said she'd be happy to take me through the house again right away, especially since it was vacant. We walked through and she agreed that the property had potential. I told her that I was going to approach the bank to see if purchasing it was an option for me.

I made an appointment with the mortgage specialist who had helped me purchase my townhome. I explained the situation, and stated that the ideal scenario would be to retain my townhome, rent it, and purchase the home. As I had some money remaining from my divorce settlement, I had a chunk of cash on hand to put down as a principal payment.

I was approved for the mortgage, under the condition that I provided the bank with a copy of a lease agreement on my townhome. I immediately placed an online ad to rent my townhome, and attracted a lovely family to rent the unit pronto. I wrote an offer on the house, another big chunk of change less than their reduced asking price. Given that there was no condition of sale on another property, and that I was proposing that we close the deal at the end of the month, the deal and the timeline was attractive to the sellers — especially since they had already been living in their new home for a few months.

I jumped quickly and got a great deal on the house. Within six weeks of looking at the "Open House" sign, I had rented my townhome furnished, and moved into the new home with our belongings and only a few pieces of furniture. After about a year of separation, I owned two homes. This wasn't what I had planned, but the process had certainly flowed beautifully.

Chica 20

Rather than jumping quickly, I think that we mistakenly try negotiating the rides that go by us – and then we miss them. The driver downshifts, brings the vehicle to a crawl, and shouts, "We're off to Shimeebaloo! Are you coming?!" And we are standing there saying, "Oh, I don't know... I would probably need to go to change my clothes and do my hair... and I would want to stop at Martha's place in Mikapoop on our way by. Can you hang out here while I get ready, drop me at Martha's on our way by, and then wait for me to visit with her? By the way, do you have the safety ratings on your vehicle handy? I just want to make sure your car will hold up in case we crash."

"Sorry," replies the driver. "Take care." And the ride passes by. I'm all for negotiating, but indecision and apathy and pokiness prevent us from jumping quickly.

What gets in the way of jumping fast? It is our habits and our mindset. We focus on what we can't do, rather than looking at what we can do. We focus on the mistakes we've made in the past, versus the possibilities of what lies ahead. We focus on what others are doing rather than what works for us. We think that we need more information, that it's not the right time, that we need more resources, that we don't have the right credentials or personality. We come up with a million reasons why it doesn't make sense to jump, rather than look at the reasons why it does makes sense to jump.

It may take some creativity to jump fast. I say creativity because who we think we are and how our life is going when the ride approaches us doesn't always seem to be a match for that potential adventure. We may think we don't have the support from our family and friends. We may think we don't have enough time or money. Or simply, we may think we are not "that kind" of person to go on that ride. But we need to be creative. Sometimes we need to just take action to be someone new, or do something new. We need to trick our minds into believing that there are more reasons to go on the ride than there are not to.

Jump High

There are times when we need to not only jump when we see an opportunity, but we need to jump high to reap the great rewards. The opportunity requires us to go above and beyond what someone else might do, and perhaps above and beyond what we have done in the past. In other words, "the best apples are at the top."

People are often asking me, "How did you make that happen Kara?" I do see myself as ambitious, but I honestly don't think that I'm a special breed. I think everyone is capable of jumping high when they choose to.

I needed to fly to San Diego for a retreat with the Evolutionary Business Council, so looked at the online classified ads to search for travel vouchers.

I found an ad stating that two vouchers were for sale for $300 ($150 each) for travel anywhere in the United States or Canada. Taxes and fees were extra, and the expiry date was quoted to be about three weeks later. The ad stated that there were no other restrictions. I reviewed the ad again, looking for anything that looked suspicious. I emailed the seller, and she confirmed that the vouchers were still available. She was located in a city about a three-hour drive away, so I asked her if she would accept an email money transfer as payment. She declined. I said that I'd get back to her as soon as I could.

Phase One: I began texting a handful of friends in the city where the seller was located to ask if my friends were in the downtown area and if they'd be up for picking up the voucher for me. A number of friends were out of town or busy, but in a few hours, I had found one friend who was up for the adventure.

As I began thinking about what to do with the second sweet travel voucher, it occurred to me that the friend who was offering to pick the vouchers up may want to use the other one. I had pre-purchased an extra ticket to the retreat in San Diego in an early bird package, so he could use the voucher and my retreat ticket. This friend had been engaged in entrepreneurial, leadership, and philanthropic activities, so the event would be a perfect opportunity for him. I called him to suggest that he take the second travel voucher and come to the event. After a short conversation, he was in for the whole shebang.

Phase Two: My friend became worried and skeptical that the travel voucher was a scam. He was suspicious of why the seller wouldn't accept an email money transfer. He was worried he would pick up and pay for the vouchers, and then the seller would turn around and book the travel (using the voucher codes) as soon as he walked away.

I searched the seller's name on social media in a few places, and she looked to be a legitimate person with a legitimate profession. I decided that I was comfortable taking the risk. I told him that I'd put my money on the line, and coached him how to confirm the voucher codes when he met the seller in person. But after a bit more correspondence with the seller, he discovered that the travel had to be completed (not just booked) by the expiry date in a few weeks, so the vouchers wouldn't work for the San Diego trip six weeks later. My friend decided against the whole shebang.

Phase Three: I needed to figure out how to pick up the travel vouchers, and decide where to take a trip in the next few weeks, in order to take advantage of this killer travel opportunity before the seller decided to make a deal with someone else.

The next morning, it occurred to me that I had pre-purchased a hotel package for Las Vegas – one of those packages where they call you and offer an incredible "one-time" deal. (I had purchased one of these packages from the same company a few years prior for New York and was impressed with the deal.) I texted my partner to ask what he thought about going to Vegas in the next few weeks. Like me, he is adventurous and spontaneous, so of course he was up for it.

I texted the seller confirming that I still wanted to take the vouchers and that I'd be in touch shortly to arrange a time and place to meet. I checked out flights, we looked at our schedules, and mapped out a 3-4 day window that we could make Vegas work. I called the hotel to make sure the hotel package could be used on the weekend we were considering.

The next question was how to make the six-hour return drive happen to pick up the travel vouchers. I needed to get there soon, before the seller decided to sell to someone else. That night, I shared with my partner that I was planning to drive the next morning to meet the seller. "It's too far," he said. He was worried about my safety, driving on winter highways. We looked at the option of purchasing flights to Vegas, but the cost was about $700 per person. We estimated that we would save about $500 by using the vouchers. I said, "You know what, $500 is worth the drive and my time. The weather is supposed to be mild. I can leave at 8:15 a.m. after I drop the kids at school, be downtown before noon to meet her, and home by 3 p.m. to pick up the kids. It's all good."

I sent a message to the seller to let her know that I could meet her the next day. Admittedly, I had a hidden hope that after I said I was going to do the six-hour drive alone that she would offer to accept an email money transfer – or, if worst case scenario it was a scam, I would at least tug at her conscience not to create a

Chica 24

situation of someone spending all day travelling to purchase a faulty voucher.

The trip the next day flowed perfectly. I was downtown before noon. As I was walking to meet the seller at our agreed upon spot, I began calling the airline so that I would have moved through the prompts and be in the queue to speak with an agent by the time I met up with her. As she was walking toward me, I had an agent from the airline on the line asking me for the voucher code. The seller handed me the vouchers, and the airline employee confirmed that the codes were valid.

We ended up paying $450 for both flights, versus the $1,400 price online. And to put a cherry on top, we scored some bonuses on the hotel. When I called to book the hotel, I asked why I had been charged an extra $70 on my credit card for the hotel package. The representative explained that I had missed the early booking bonus, but since I had now booked my package, they would refund me as a courtesy. There was another $70 back in my pocket! Then the representative informed me that with the hotel package we would be receiving VIP tickets for dinner and a show for one evening of our stay. Wow!

A 6-hour road trip wasn't in my plans for that week, and Vegas wasn't in my plans for the next month, but we scored a killer deal, and it turned out to be a wonderful adventure from start to finish. I had never been to Vegas, and it made sense to me to ride the beautiful flow and simply relish in the gift.

There's something to be said for being willing to jump high and do what others are not. Now, this doesn't mean that we take risks blindly or do things that are against our values. We can go above and beyond to capitalize on opportunities that appear before us, and then simply be proud that we had the courage and determination to pull it off, and relish in the happiness that we create for ourselves.

Keep Jumping

One of Napoleon Hill's famous tales is about mining for gold in the days of the gold rush. A man named Darby set out to find gold, and indeed made a discovery with his pick and shovel. He covered up his treasure, and left to fetch his uncle and some equipment to mine the gold. The two men returned and mined one car of ore, but as they continued mining were horrified that the vein of gold disappeared. They stopped, sold the equipment, and returned home. However, the man who they sold their equipment to investigated the site they had abandoned, only to discover that they had hit a fault line and stopped mining three feet from millions of dollars of gold.

See, the challenge we face in life is that we never really know when we are three feet away. We may be seven feet away or one foot away. Sometimes that jackpot is just at our fingertips, but we can't see it. I certainly believe in the law of attraction, and have tremendous appreciation for synchronicity, but I'm also a firm believer that hard work and diligence pays off. We need to keep going even when we don't know how far we are from success.

I surround myself with coaches and peeps who encourage me to keep jumping when I get disillusioned or tired. One of my coaches, Andrea Carter of Wealthy Woman Warrior, says to me regularly, "Keep going, Kara!" I want to be completely candid and say that there are moments and days when I question myself. As a self-published author, the costs of producing a book are tremendous. I spend weeks creating material for my programs without an immediate pot of gold to collect. That said, I do what I do because I believe so passionately in making a difference, and because I hear from the people I work with the tremendous changes they make in their life, and the incredible happiness they create when they work with me. I know that I need to keep on jumping, and that eventually I will be rewarded for my diligence and hard work.

Sometimes we need to persist in order to show the universe that we really want something, rather than quitting. We need to remind ourselves that even when we can't see the finish line, the cost of quitting is usually much, much higher than the rewards of keeping on.

Jump Over Hurdles

A hurdle doesn't always indicate that something isn't "meant to be." A hurdle is just a hurdle. They are part of the journey. They simply appear. Have you ever watched an Olympic athlete jump over hurdles? It is as if they float over the barricades. We can do this in life too.

When I flew to San Diego for the Evolutionary Business Council retreat, I booked my flight using points. I had three flights, and two connections – flying from 5 p.m. to 1 a.m. So, first and foremost here, let's bring attention to the fact that I chose to use my points and to book the milk run to San Diego rather than pay for a more direct flight.

The first flight, which was only 30 minutes to a nearby city, departed half an hour late. Apparently the airport in our destination city had just implemented a new air traffic flow policy the day before. As we sat on the runway, I could feel my neighbor becoming increasingly annoyed. I took the opportunity to get some more texts and emails done before we were in the air, with no wifi connection.

In the next city, I followed the "Connections" signs. I walked for about five minutes, got to my gate, and realized that there was no food near the gate. Given that it was 6:30 p.m. and I had been busy that day working, tidying the house, packing, and tying up loose ends for a five-day and seven-person child care plan, I'd only had a few snacks throughout the day. I was getting pretty "hangry" (hungry and angry). I promptly turned around, walked back quickly where I had come from, and ordered a sandwich. With my sandwich tucked in my purse, I returned to the gate.

What I discovered when back at where I thought I needed to be was that there was a set of glass doors separating me from the gate. The first time there I had quickly spotted the gate, behind a set of glass doors. I had seen two security guards standing in front of the glass doors, and had assumed that I would show the guards my boarding pass for them to let me through the glass doors to the gate. Now, looking at the gate on the other side of the glass doors, I could see that the last of the passengers in line to board were handing their boarding passes to the attendant.

The guards informed me that I had to go all the way back out to the main concourse of the airport, re-enter through the United States customs entrance, and go through security again. We exchanged a look of anxiety as we observed the last few passengers handing over their boarding passes. I started running down the hallway, and the security guard ran beside me telling me directions on how to proceed. Bless his heart. Ten minutes later, after the fastest customs and security process possible, and as my name was being called over the intercom, I arrived on the other side (the right side) of the glass doors. Even though I didn't have time to pee, I had my dinner and I was thankful that I had made the flight.

As I walked down the corridor and approached the flight attendant standing at the head of the plane, I noticed another

Chica 28

employee walking behind me holding a few bag tags in his hand. I looked at the dreaded stickers and knew what he had in mind. Sure enough, after a minute of lurking behind me, he said, "There isn't room for your carry-on luggage on the plane. I'm going to have to check it for you." I looked down at my little suitcase and pleadingly asked, "Are you sure? I'm really not keen on checking it. Anytime I've checked it, it has come out damaged." He looked at me empathetically and asked the flight attendant standing at the head of the plane if there was a place for my luggage. She said there wasn't, and assured me there wouldn't be a problem with checking my suitcase. Now looking at her pleadingly, I said, "If there's anywhere at all that you could put it onboard, I'd really appreciate it." Another attendant chimed into the conversation and mentioned a few seat numbers that were empty. She suggested we put my luggage under one of those seats.

Hurdles of all kinds – big and small – pop up in life all the time. But at the end of the day, we can jump over hurdles like an Olympic athlete when we:

1. Give up complaining and getting mad – at people and circumstances.

2. Get creative – and look at what we can do, rather than what we can't do.

3. Take accountability – and look at what we could've done.

4. Be calm and respectful – as we deal with hurdles.

5. Practice being proactive – by considering what we've learned for dealing with future hurdles.

In any situation, it is easy to fall victim to a hurdle. We point the finger at somebody or something. Generally, we don't like to admit that we had anything to do with a situation going sideways. Rather than focusing on how to jump over the hurdle like an Olympic athlete, we get caught up in stories and blaming.

As I crawled past my neighbors into my window seat, with my bladder full and my forehead, armpits, and crotch sweaty from running, I caught myself being mad at the airline for being late. Wait, no, I decided that I was mad at the air traffic control people who had made the plane late. Then I was mad at the airport because the signage had not properly directed me to customs and security.

But the truth was that I had booked the milk run journey with connections. I failed to read the signs properly. And I had chosen to backtrack in the airport to find dinner even with a short connection time – I could have chosen to buy food on the plane. In fact, knowing my hangry tendencies, I should have packed a snack to have on hand in case I was tight on time.

We need to resist the downhill spiral of getting annoyed, grumpy or even nasty to the people we encounter as we strive to jump over hurdles. I do believe that when we are testy with people, this negativity creates ill emotional and physical health in our bodies, and that the negativity ends up returning to us in karma at some point.

As I zipped through customs and security in record time that night, I was struck by the number of people who I interacted with that a temperamental traveller may have blasted frustration at – but these people were all just doing their job. The security guards on the wrong side of the glass, the U.S. pre-screening customs officer who made sure I had filled out the form properly, the customs officer who asked me five different but similar questions about where I was going, the line of security officers who screened my items, the airline employees who tried to put my luggage beneath the plane. In truth, they are all people who are employed to be in service of people travelling. At a number of points in moving through the security steps, when I was about to be a crab pot and say something out of frustration, I bit my lip and simply said, "I'm in a hurry and need to catch my flight. Thank you so much." I believe that my ability to remain calm and respectful is what helped me jump that hurdle in miracle time.

When we deal with hurdles in this way – by giving up whining, being proactive, taking accountability, remaining courteous, and learning from our experiences, life certainly feels more flowful (yes, I made that word up). We enhance our inner sense of power because we assure ourselves that we have the strength and skill to deal with the hurdles that pop up. Rather than being at the mercy of challenge after challenge, we see that we are on an adventure to figure out how we can use our own power to move over hurdles like an Olympic athlete.

Flow Gracefully

Sometimes we jump in life and land rather awkwardly. Sometimes we sprain our ankle. Sometimes we crash and burn. Sometimes the crash and burn looks like a belly flop into the pool, and sometimes the crash and burn looks like a big cannon ball into a pool without water.

I don't think that flowing gracefully means that we'll avoid hurdles and epic fails. We're only human after all. In fact, many of the world's most eminent thought leaders believe that the bigger your failures, the more you grow. It's not the hurdle or epic fail that matters, it's what we do afterwards that really matters.

When river water flows, the stream may crash over a boulder, free fall down a cliff, or meander through banks; regardless, this is all flow... and a powerful energy and intention drive the water toward the ocean no matter what the flow looks like. In parallel, I believe that regardless of the path that we are on in life, we need to maintain our own powerful energy and intentions. We need to commit to following our passions so that we flow over hurdles and live out our mission. Despite what seem to be imperfect decisions and actions in our own minds, we need to keep living intentionally.

When you believe that everything has a purpose in life, and that you can flow through life by learning and growing no matter the obstacle, a hurdle simply looks like something to flow over.

I've certainly had my own epic fails. I recently cheated on my partner. Tall, dark, and handsome, the new guy seemed to give promise of being the perfect lover, perfect dad, perfect businessman, and perfect housekeeper. Before I found out what size he is "down there," I had to stop myself in continuing to jeopardize the core of my integrity.

At first, I justified my indiscretion, and then I was extremely shameful. I had never cheated in a relationship ever before. Honestly, I had never even been tempted to cheat in a relationship because my values of honor and commitment are so strong. I had to commit to learn and grow through the experience, and look at what this was all saying about me at a deeper level.

I began to see it all as a blessing in our relationship, and part of my journey. My partner and I were moved to have conversations – to share deep thoughts and feelings – that we had been avoiding. Over the following months, my partner and I unravelled and explored the progression of our relationship, and what we had each done to contribute to getting to that point.

I reminded myself that experiences like this are a blessing for me to flow through because of my mission to coach people to create extraordinary lives. Infidelity is a common experience that couples face, and I have now experienced infidelity on both sides of the fence so to speak. I believe that my path in life reveals significant and challenging life experiences so that I can truly relate to the people I coach.

My partner and I separated, and in the months following our separation, I was dealing with: securing financing and completing the purchase of our joint home; self-representing myself in a legal matter; my grandmother passing away; travelling to Mexico to support my partner in last visits with his terminally ill mother; addressing a flood in my rental property; evicting a tenant who was not paying his rent in my other rental property; working four days a week; and of course being a mom. I was also working diligently to finish this book. Throughout these months, I simply focused on the opportunity to learn and grow, to maintain my commitment to my writing mission, and to enhance my ability to flow in life with peace and ease despite my circumstances.

Stamina is earned. The ability to deal powerfully with life circumstances while moving onward requires practice. As we enhance our skills to persist, we build our capacity to deal with adversity and complications. Then even as the hurdles get higher in life, we have the ability to keep clearing them.

Whether a stream flows gently underground toward the ocean, or down the steep and rocky side of a mountain toward the ocean, it's all flow in a beautiful, purposeful, and unique way. Blood, pain, hurt, and trauma can be absorbed and cleansed in the rivers as we journey on our path of intention. We can whirlpool in the face of conflict and come out stronger. A rock can be thrown into the midst of our flow and we can carry on our path of intention and purpose. Our ability to move gracefully with the flow of life is what fuels peace of mind, internal power, resilience, and meaningful results.

Ellen Rogin on...
Jump!

> "The one thing I do that nobody else does is jump three and four times for one rebound."

> DENNIS RODMAN

I still remember one day when I was out for a walk in San Diego, when I bumped into Ellen Rogin – who was also attending the Evolutionary Business Council retreat. She was coming out of the drug store that I was going into. I asked Ellen what she was up to, and she said that she was snagging some affordably-priced snacks for the airport and her flight home. I chuckled appreciatively and thought, "A woman after my heart."

Ellen radiates warmth, and a down-to-earth presence. She is a role model for dreaming big, while acknowledging the realities of life. She is clear about her mission on this planet, and committed to her family. She is massively successful, and also extremely humble.

Ellen's New York Times bestselling book *Picture Your Prosperity: Smart Money Moves to Turn Your Vision into Reality* and her TedX video "The Surprising Way to Teach Your Kids to be

Smart with Money" have captured the attention of tens of thousands of people around the world.

~

Ellen grew up in the northern suburbs of Chicago. Her two parents supported her in what she wanted to do. Her dad owned an architectural firm. Her mom was well educated, and had a few jobs (but didn't really have anything to do with her family's finances). When Ellen went off to college, her mom trained to be a tour guide and started her own company. Her parents paid for Ellen's college, and they encouraged her to travel. She says that, all in all, she's grateful that she didn't really have any major challenges to overcome growing up. She truly appreciates her parents, who loved her, supported her, and encouraged her to do whatever she set her mind to.

Ellen comments, "I think about how important it is what you tell yourself, and what you've been told about yourself. Especially when it's positive, it can be really instructive and impactful."

When her family travelled to Acapulco when she was five years old, Ellen's mom said, "You're such a good traveller." This shaped Ellen's identity, and led her to travel substantially herself. She says that she did the same thing with her own children – praising them for being good travellers. "Our minds are so powerful," Ellen affirms. "We truly can use positive affirmations to create what we want in life."

After completing her education in economics and accounting, she began her career in public accounting – which she hated! Next, she moved into financial planning. Although she wasn't sure if she'd like it, or be good at financial planning, Ellen thought, "Well if I don't, then at least I'll know how to manage my own money!"

Ellen's father told her, "You'll work for these guys for awhile, and then start your own firm." Ellen remembers thinking that she didn't see herself starting a business. Sure enough, Ellen started her own financial planning firm at age 28, with one part-time employee. Ellen notes she is extremely grateful that she had great role models and great encouragers.

She gained clients and grew her firm by speaking and teaching at networking events, non-profit events, and so on. She recognized early that she loved what she was doing, and appreciated that she could have an impact on more people by public speaking, than she could have working with people one-on-one.

Through the 90s, Ellen had a strong desire to write books and speak on large stages. She was also building her financial planning firm. But her big goals of writing and speaking weren't unfolding for her; she was talking about it, but it just wasn't happening.

She admits that at the time she felt inauthentic and defeated. Years later, after looking back and doing some introspective work about what was really going on, Ellen saw that she had conflicting goals. Most important to her was to build her company, and to be there for her young children. Speaking would have taken her away from both. "What I thought I wanted to do just didn't match what my real priorities were."

She believes that it's not possible to find perfect "balance" in life – it is more important to set priorities, give your full attention to those priorities, and realize that your focus isn't going to be permanent.

"At different stages in our life, we can choose different priorities. I wouldn't have believed it when my kids were little, but boom! Really, you blink your eyes and your kids are grown."

One important parenting lesson came early for her.

"We live in an area with a lot of stay-at-home moms. I'd be dropping my daughter at preschool, and I realized that it wasn't just my kid who was having separation anxiety."

Ellen still remembers that when she stopped feeling guilty about dropping her daughter off at preschool, her daughter stopped crying. As her kids grew, and were in grade school, she started to feel guilty that she wasn't there more with them.

"Then, over time, I saw that I was at more events with my kids than some of the stay-at-home moms." Ellen acknowledges that everyone is simply doing the best they can, and making different choices, in raising their children.

She chose priorities that spoke to her, while other people choose different routes.

For instance, nurturing her health and fitness has always been a priority for her; it has always been clear to her that in order to take good care of her family, she needs to take good care of herself.

Her house, on the other hand, wasn't always clean and organized. And, Ellen acknowledges that she didn't spend a lot of time with friends. She didn't chat on the phone or go out for coffees and lunches with friends, because she wanted to get work done.

This, unfortunately, led to resentment and some sadness for the time she never spent with friends.

But she learned to "let it go."

Today, she goes away every year on a trip with a group of girlfriends who have been friends for many years (most whom were stay-at-home moms). On the early trips, her girlfriends would talk about what they were doing with their kids and with their friends. Ellen noticed that she was envious that her girlfriends seemed to have large circles of friends. She had to keep reminding herself of what her priorities were. "I know how important friend-time is because it rejuvenates me, but when I look back, what I also know is that I chose the perfect path for me."

Even though Ellen was working full-time, she wanted to be present and attentive to her kids. When she was home, she focused on her kids and creating pockets of fun. They would do activities at home like dance contests. "Now my kids roll their eyes at me and say, 'Mom, that was stupid.' But I think it was really was fun." When her children got older, their family travelled, which fed Ellen's goals to spend quality time with her kids and her husband. She wanted her kids to experience travel adventures. "I made time for my kids when it was important," shares Ellen proudly.

Marriage also needs to be a top priority, she insists. "I think when my kids were little and I was working so much, I didn't pay enough attention to the importance of my marriage as I should've. Luckily we made it through."

The key in marriage, she found, is to take personal responsibility.

"There were times when I could be really blamey of my husband... and then the second I looked at what my part was, it made things much better. When our children were little, it seemed at the time that my husband made a unilateral decision to leave his job and start investing in real estate – which did not bring in any income at the time. All of a sudden, I was in charge of making all the money. I was incredibly angry. But when I realized that being angry wasn't going to help anyone, I started looking at what I could do. With this shift in mindset, my business grew like crazy. I'm grateful now because I see that I jumped and expanded my business in ways that would not have happened if he hadn't quit his job."

It wasn't quick and easy to get to this calm and accepting place with her husband. As Ellen's parents had a very traditional marriage (her dad went off to work and her mom was home most of her childhood), her internal picture was one of a husband being in charge of the money. Now, being a financial expert, Ellen realized that this "picture" was ridiculous. It did take her much time to realize this is why she was initially so uncomfortable with the situation.

She needed to move past blame, and embrace personal responsibility. She needed to look at what her part was, and focus on what she could do to move forward.

She could accept being the breadwinner, or she could be angry and unhappy. Ellen chose happy, which has worked beautifully for her, her marriage, and her family.

For some of her friends and clients, coming to terms with being in charge of the family earnings is often a challenge for women. Many women, despite knowing there are relationships where the woman earns significantly more money, still take time to adjust to this. "Many of us were brought up watching movies and TV, where it was the man in charge of supporting the family. It can take some personal growth to move past these Hollywood images of how things are 'supposed to be.'"

Ellen kept jumping and worked diligently to grow her financial advisory practice, and also grew within herself.

She explains that, in the past, when she would evaluate her annual business goals at the end of the year, she would see that her business had advanced, but not on par with her targets.

Finally, she recognized that she had a subconscious belief of, "I never meet my business goals." Her friend Candy Barone says, "If you spot it, you got it." In other words, if you recognize that you are carrying an unarticulated negative belief, guaranteed it's playing out in your life. "Not meeting my business goals was exactly what was showing up for me. I had to do some work on that belief."

In turn, that shifted her internal dialogue to, "I always meet my business goals." Soon after recognizing the subconscious belief, and committing to shift her thought pattern, she had much better results.

These shifts do not require years of therapy. "Sometimes it's just a matter of seeing that what you are saying to yourself is not what you want to have happen."

It was also a learning curve about focus and perseverance. Ellen's first book took longer than expected to publish. It took her making a firm decision to step up, and get focused, in order to get it done. She was nudged along by her then 10-year-old daughter Amy, asking, "Mom are you going to ever finish your book?" Ellen realized that she was embarrassed about talking about writing a book, and wanted to actually have written a book.

It was around 2010 that Ellen became clearer that her passion and mission is to help women be more comfortable, empowered, and optimistic about their money. She began working with financial advisors to train them to be better with working with their female clients. She worked with a large mutual fund company to help create a personal finance workshop for women. And, because her business and kids grew to the point that she could be away more, she began speaking and travelling more.

When Lisa Kueng and Ellen began talking about writing *Picture Your Prosperity* in 2012, they set an intention for the book to hit the New York Times bestseller list. They truly believed that the information they had to share was needed in the world, and would have a significant impact on people. Each time the two ladies would begin to get scared about their goal, and next steps, they would focus on why they were writing the book. They wanted to jump high and create a big platform, so that they could reach, and help, a massive number of people. *Picture Your Prosperity* was released in 2015, and it did hit the New York Times bestseller list.

There is something to be said for divine timing, says Ellen. "All of those years of work and experience in building my financial planning business got me ready to do a better job of the writing and speaking that I always wanted to do."

"I am grateful for my career, and that I'm living out my mission. I've started to notice the kids of the stay-at-home moms are going off to college, and the moms are trying to figure out what's next for them. They've been laid off from their only job of being a mom. They are in a challenging phase of their lives."

Though there are some regrets, and some things she'd do over if she could, overall she believes her children were raised well.

"Our kids always felt loved and important. That's something that was always really important to me and my husband, and I think that means a lot," she notes.

"Being a working mom did not negatively impact their ability to be happy, functional people. In their case, it helped them grow into who they are today."

Some people say you can have it all, and some people say you can't have it all. Ellen thinks that you should have what you most want. Time goes by so fast, so you need to get clear about your current direction, and what you most value, and be open to making changes over time.

You need to: 1) be clear about your vision of success and be willing to jump for it; 2) focus on the value that you give to others; 3) identify your priorities; 4) spot negative subconscious beliefs so that they don't hold you back; and 5) trust that there is a bigger picture, and that everything will work out in perfect time.

~

Ellen's words of wisdom certainly ring true for me. There isn't a day that goes by when I don't feel pulled in different directions: my kids, my other half, my work, my health, my extended family, etc.

But I remind myself to keep focusing on doing the best I can to be a good mom, a good partner, and a good citizen of the world.

What gives me pure joy and hope is that there are more and more people, like Ellen, who are committed to role model creating happiness, learning, and generosity in their lives – which is what is absolutely required to create a tipping point toward positivity on this planet.

Be Powerful

"Be Impeccable With Your Word. Speak with integrity. Say only what you mean. Avoid using the word to speak against yourself or to gossip about others. Use the power of your word in the direction of truth and love."

DON MIGUEL RUIZ

I'd like to explore what "being powerful" means in the way of mastering ourselves – being internally calm, confident, courageous, committed, and connected. We are talking about the power of our thoughts, words, and actions. We are talking about our inner strength and our integrity.

Being powerful is often thought of as controlling or domineering others; it's a common belief that we can get more and have more, if we are powerful in commanding others to act. We set out to learn about negotiation, marketing, psychology, and other disciplines in order to understand how other people think and behave so that we can shift them.

But what if us being kind, enthusiastic, sexy, empathetic, generous, patient, supportive, grateful, and dedicated packs so much punch, that we naturally empower others to be this way too? What if we inspire people to be kind, enthusiastic, generous, patient, supportive, grateful, and dedicated because of who we are? What if our leadership subconsciously leads them to think and behave in this positive way?

I believe that as we become highly effective in our own lives, we enhance our faith in ourselves to do the right thing and create results; naturally, then, others take notice, want to be close to our energy, and want to experience the same level of happiness and effectiveness in their own lives. As we become more connected to our passions and mission, people in our lives will want to bend over backwards for us because of who we are and what we are up to. They may even want to join in our adventures and projects; they may be lit up and create their own.

When you are grounded, and full of energy and passion, the positive energy that exudes from you attracts more positivity. You can create a positive spiral upwards with your attitude, relationships, and results. You can move mountains.

Let the Story Go

We can choose to use the capacity of our mind to move with the natural flow of life and powerfully attract magic... or we can choose to be mired in the overwhelming and dramatic stories of people, life events, and circumstances. We can put our focus on our intentions, goals, and next action steps... or we can chitter-chatter and daydream about how life could be or should be. I do believe in the power of the two former approaches. However, I have found over the years that it has taken me being open to coaching, and consciously and consistently choosing this way of life.

I believe that the key to staying in power, and staying out of drama in life, is to separate the facts ("what is") from our interpretations and embellishments (the reality TV version of "what is"). These are the movies that play through our mind, and the sensational episodes that we broadcast – where we blame other people for saying and doing awful things, speak about sickness and unfortunate events, complain about financial hardship and losses, lament about the systems that dictate our lives, and describe in detail conflict-ridden relationships. We talk about our own drama and describe others' drama, and once we are through sharing about the drama we already know of, we inquire how things are going with X, Y, and Z so that we can learn new drama.

This can be hard because so many people in society feed off of drama. In a weird way, sometimes people want to be assured that their life is okay, because what someone else is dealing with in their life is worse. Some people are so addicted to reading newspapers and tabloids, watching television, etc. that they crave drama and seek it out everywhere they go. It's a subconscious addiction to drama.

Like teaching a child to chew with her/his mouth closed, or training a puppy not to beg for food at the table, we need to commit to a "no-drama personal policy" and then commit to implement it. We need to continue catching ourselves creating stories in our minds that generate unnecessary negativity. Step away from those things that fuel and amplify emotions, and complicate situations.

Tenting

When my partner and I first started dating, he shared that he enjoys camping. He looked at me eagerly, gauging my body language as a response. I replied, "Honestly, I'm not a camper. Even when I was a toddler and was camping with my parents, I made it known that I thought camping was dirty and stinky. I like a flush toilet, hot shower, and stove...very comfortable cabin-style nature experiences. Oh, and I get cranky when I'm cold." I could see the disappointment in his eyes. He continued to share that he likes a night of camping, and a good hike the next day, followed by a refreshing stay in a hotel. As the conversation progressed, I said, "Well, never say 'never'. I'll try it once with you."

Our first camping outing went well. On a Saturday morning, he texted me to ask what I was up to for the day. I responded with a few low-key things I had on the go, and asked what he had in mind. He said he was thinking a trip to the mountains. "Today?" I asked. "Maybe," he responded. I did some quick calling to hotels in the area. They were booked, and what was left was pricey. I reported by text the hotel options that were full, and the hotel options that were still available. "Or...we could camp?!" he suggested. I took a deep breath, and responded, "Sure." I informed him that he was in charge – of the gear, the set-up, and anything else that went along with camping.

We took his son on the trip. The drive was beautiful, and we saw wildlife at the side of the road. We broke up the 3.5-hour drive by stopping for pizza along the way. We pulled into town at about 7 p.m. and looked for a campsite. We drove around and looked at what seemed like hundreds of sites. When he asked me what I thought of a site, I'd say, "You're in charge. Whatever you think." It wasn't a cover-up. He really was in charge. I know nothing about camping. We set up the tent and went into town for dinner.

Chica 48

The following day, we had lunch at a local restaurant, walked around a stunning waterfall site, and then dragging our feet, got in the car to go home. The trip seemed way too short.

When we returned, I shared with my mom that we'd embarked on a camping adventure, and that the trip had gone well. She said she was glad she didn't know that we were tenting, as she would have been worried about bears. "In the fall, the bears are starting to get pretty hungry," she explained. I agreed with her and laughed, "Well, I'm glad too that we didn't talk. It's better that I didn't get the bears heads up."

Two weeks later, my partner said that he wanted to go back to the mountains for a festival, and to see a keynote presentation by astronaut Chris Hadfield. I agreed, thinking we could do another trip the three of us. When I realized that I would be with my two kids that weekend, I asked him if he wanted to take his son on his own, or go all together. "Sure, let's take the zoo," he said. Up to that point, for nine months, we had mainly focused on building our relationship. The five of us had done one activity together – a rodeo one summer afternoon for a few hours. Without saying it, we both recognized that this was the next step to take. What a curious adventure this could be!

We packed the three kids in the back of my Mazda 3, and stuffed the hatchback trunk with the tent, sleeping bags, pillows, mats, one bag of food, backpacks, and headed out. About five hours later, as we approached town, I spotted a black bear on the side of the highway. I could hear my mom's voice in my head, "The bears are hungry this time of year." We arrived in town in time for my partner and his son to catch the latter part of Chris Hadfield's keynote presentation. Then we grabbed dinner, and finally headed to the campground – the only one still open that late in the season.

We pulled into the campground at about 11 p.m. with all three kids sleeping in the back. He set up the tent and told me to make a fire — which, yes, I can do. We then transferred the kids to the tent and they continued sleeping. The two of us hung around the fire, had a few glasses of wine, and engaged in our usual light and entertaining banter. He mentioned that the tent was crowded, and that we could just sleep in the car. As much as camping car sex would have been a hoot, I stated firmly that I didn't think it was wise to leave a 5, 7, and 10-year-old sleeping alone in a tent in the wilderness. He said that he could sleep in the car, and I stated that I didn't think that it would be a wise move on his part to leave all of us in the tent alone, especially given that he is the "camper." It had been a big work week for me, so at about 2 a.m. I said that I needed to head to bed. A disappointed and annoyed look crossed his face. "Just stay up with me for another bit," he said. From past experience, I had come to know that could mean an hour or two or three. I declined, and he said in an annoyed tone, "Fine, go."

I crawled into a cold sleeping bag and focused on moving my thoughts away from worrying if the kids were warm. My heavy eyes and tired body took over my mind, and I fell asleep... probably for about half an hour, until I woke from being cold. Of course, immediately my mind jumped to thoughts of bears being hungry at this time of year. My emotions started to skyrocket. I was lying in a tent cold and with three children around me. I didn't even like tenting. I began to get angry at my partner for not being better prepared and looking after us. Then I recognized that I did NOT want this story of my partner being an inconsiderate, ill-prepared jerk to get any bigger. I reminded myself that stories and emotions and blame of this nature has turned me into a grumpy, resentful witch for days, weeks, and sometimes months. I've committed in my life not to live like this. I needed to take my own advice and get into action. So I got up and decided to go get warm by the fire.

Chica 50

After I had gotten my contacts back on my eyes, got out of the tent, and got my shoes on, I realized that my partner was not at the fire. I glanced over at the car and saw him sleeping inside. My story and emotions skyrocketed from a 5/10 to a 10/10. I marched over to the car, swung open the driver's door, grabbed his shoulders and shook him. "Wake up!! Wake up!!" I said. "What?!" he mumbled in a sleepy spaced out tone. "Who are you?" he drawled. "Are you kidding me??!!" I yelled in response. (I'm pretty sure I started yelling at this point.) My story and emotions moved up a notch to an 11/10. I stormed off to get the fire going again and stood by it, hovering over the small flame that was eagerly working to catch on the fresh wood I had stacked on.

A few moments later, my partner crawled out of the car. He shuffled tiredly over to the fire and began stacking heaps of wood on it. He asked me what I was upset about. I informed him that I was cold, and that the one with the survival skills (him) was sleeping in the car. He kept putting logs on the fire. He reiterated that the tent was crowded and admitted that he has a "thing" with being claustrophobic. I suggested that I sleep in the car and he sleep in the tent with the kids. We continued talking and he explained to me that most bears don't attack at night. He proceeded to inform me what to do if I was faced with a bear ready to attack at night. He explained the difference between brown and black bears, and how to react when faced with a black bear or a brown bear. He then told me backwoods camping stories of being surrounded by wolves. As we both grew warm and even more tired, he encouraged me to go back into the tent – he would go into the car. I couldn't believe that this conversation had gone in circles so many times. I suggested that if the tent was still too crowded with him and the three kids in there, that I would grab my two kids and sleep in the car with them – he and his son could sleep in the tent. I reiterated that he had two choices: sleep in the tent with his son while we slept in the car, or sleep in the tent with all of us. He chose the latter.

This is the type of situation that would have put me into a witchy frenzy for days or weeks years ago, but I didn't let it happen. My former self would have stewed about what a jerk he was. I would have told all my friends and family what a jerk he was. I would have either given him the silent treatment or the cold shoulder for days. And then I would've reminded him what a jerk he is for weeks, maybe months... okay, maybe years. By taking action, by going to the fire and then waking him up, I committed to myself not to suffer and continue building a resentful and blameful story.

At the end of the day, creating and holding onto a negative and dramatic story doesn't do anyone any good. The person holding onto the story and being a grumpy witch – and the people who hear about the story and have to deal with a grumpy witch – are all in a yucky mindset and energy.

The Friend

I noticed one day that I had not been in touch with a close friend for some time. Over a period of a few years, we had become increasingly closer. We would text daily or at least weekly about life updates. If I had something particularly difficult to deal with, I would call him to bounce the situation off of him. He knows me so well – my cherished values, what I stand for, how I'm committed to making a difference, what I've been through in the last five years, how I've learned and grown. He also knows my hang-ups and will call me out on bad behavior in a gentle but powerful way; he'll support me to figure out what I need to do next and get back on

Chica 52

track. Over time, we had even commented that it seemed we were like brother and sister.

Given the time that had passed since we last connected, I caught myself starting to formulate a story, and get enraptured in it. I was hypothesizing the reasons that he hadn't been in touch, thinking about what I may have done or not done to upset him. Really, I have to admit at a deeper level (nobody wants to admit this kind of stuff), that I was feeling abandoned, like an unloved five-year-old child. (For the record, I need to say that I was never an abandoned, unloved five-year-old child, but it's crazy how our minds can play tricks on us and subconsciously create deep seeded and amplified emotions that have no merit.)

See, another important piece in this story is that I had also become quite close with another male friend through the same time period. We would go for coffee or a drink and have great conversations about what we were really dealing with personally and professionally. The combination of our personalities and genders helped us to support each other in offering different perspectives and ideas.

Because I had met both guy friends in the same personal development course, we all knew each other and shared a connection. The two guys had started biking and skiing together. Sometimes the three of us would meet for a coffee or drink here and there, and chat about life.

After a few years of lovely friendship, I received a call from the wife of the second friend I mentioned above. His wife had shared candidly and vulnerably that she had an issue with me. She found me to be insincere, and inadvertently she shared that she was uncomfortable with the time I was spending with her husband.

As I was thinking about the first friend I mentioned above, and missing him, it occurred to me that the timeline from which we last saw each other lined up fairly well to the timeline from which I had spoken to my other friend's wife, and decided not to spend any more time with him. I began to wonder, "Did they talk? Does the other wife now have an issue with me too?" My friend had mentioned that they had gone camping together with their wives. Maybe somehow it had been decided that I shouldn't be friends with either of the guys.

I decided that everything I was daydreaming about was conjecture, and that I wasn't going to let a story that I was manufacturing in my mind get in the way of a cherished friend, especially when I had just lost one. I texted my friend and asked, "Quick coffee or wine this weekend?"

"Sure!" he responded promptly. My body relaxed and I felt relieved.

When we met for coffee and snagged a table in the very busy coffee shop, I acknowledged, "I've been so busy in the last few months, and I realized the other day that I miss you." We had a wonderful chat about what was new in his life, and what was new in mine. I left the coffee shop feeling reconnected with him, and full of fresh energy and optimism to take on the work I needed to accomplish during the rest of my day.

Had I let that story that was building in my mind and heart sit and fester, I probably would not have taken the step to ask my friend out for coffee. I could easily have blamed him for not being in touch with me, especially given that it was around the launch of my first book – wasn't it completely obvious that this was a time I needed support and encouragement from my friends? (Or maybe he thought that I was busy and on top of the world, celebrating my accomplishment.) Instead, I chose to simply focus on the fact that I was missing him. And without the story and emotion, what would you do about missing someone? Ask to see them of course! It seems simple, yet the way we often live and allow our relationships to play out is so much more dramatic and complicated.

And are you wondering about the second friend? We don't spend time together anymore. I do miss him, and honestly, there is a grain of resentment in me that I lost a wonderful friend. At the same time, it doesn't serve me to make up and tell stories about the reasons we don't see each other anymore. While I have some information that leads me to believe that there is way more to the story, it just doesn't matter. It is what it is.

Letting go of our stories is a constant commitment and practice. Believe me, it's something that I am constantly working on. I am always checking in with myself and reflecting on the extent to which I am being realistic and authentic about what is going on in my life, and the extent to which I am embellishing, complaining, and being overly emotional.

Most importantly, keep your thoughts and stories as simple as possible. You can give people a list of what you've been dealing with: your dog died, your car needs a new windshield wiper, your child has chicken pox, you owe $2,000 in income tax, you got a bad haircut, your basement flooded, and your great aunt lost her job. Or you can say you've had a lot going on. The truth is, everyone has a lot going on. Some people just talk about it more than others.

And equally important, be realistic and focus on the action you need to take. A rainy day isn't a terrible day. It is simply a wet day... so grab some rubber boots and an umbrella as you walk out the door. A mother-in-law who constantly gives you advice on cooking, housecleaning, and parenting isn't a horrible person; she's normal. Do your best to limit alone time with her, ask your husband for support, and implement one piece of her advice so she feels needed and appreciated. If your ex is paying a lawyer thousands of dollars to recuperate a few hundred dollars from you for expenses related to your children's activities (even when he has been underpaying you in child support), pay a visit to the courthouse to inquire what free or low-cost programs may be available to help you resolve the issue. Or ask your brother's lawyer friend for a huge favor, and get some advice. Be grateful for the money you are receiving, and be grateful for the learning experience, and the opportunity to practice being proactive and assertive.

At the end of the day, our stories drain our energy when we can simply make a choice not to give them space in our lives. We lose sleep over them. We waste precious time creating them, building them, talking about them, dwelling on them when we could be setting goals, dreaming big, taking action, helping others.

To let go of our stories, we need to get really honest about the impact our stories have on us, and the types of negative relationships that we create around our stories. The practice of letting go of the drama can be like yoga – we can absolutely enhance our flexibility, balance, and strength little by little, but we need to continually commit to get ourselves out the door to the yoga studio and to continually commit to "up" our skill level.

Notice Expectations

Expectations are founded on the stories that we create in our mind about how we think life should unfold. We create an ideal scenario in our mind, often subconsciously – based on our upbringing, our past experiences, or a figment of our imagination (perhaps even based on media messages). We create these daydreams, sometimes in a moment or sometimes over time, usually without even realizing it.

While they teach us in communication books to articulate to other people how their behavior and events didn't meet our expectations, I think it's even more powerful to proactively prevent and manage our expectations so that we are less likely to be impacted by others. We remain in power on our own accord. Here are a few tips for keeping expectations in check:

- Because it's often a subconscious story, we need to practice noticing when we are building a story before something has even happened.

- We can then think about what could work well (potential blessings), and what might not work well (potential challenges). Preparing and putting backstops in place for obstacles can be beneficial. This sets us up to be ready to roll with a variety of different scenarios that could play out.

- As events unfold, we need to notice when we are getting emotional when a situation is not playing out how we thought it would. We can focus on what is really happening and take it for what it is, as opposed to resentfully compare what is happening with our story of what should happen.

- If we notice a trend of being disappointed about the same theme, it may mean our needs aren't being met. If it's a repeated situation, and you can identify that there is an element of the story or expectation that is actually really important to you, it's good to have the conversation to articulate what's important and why.

- Lastly, but probably most importantly, I believe we can simply allow ourselves less energy and space to generate expectations. The busier we are in life, and the more focused we are on our mission and passions, the less time we have to daydream and build up expectations.

I'm continually working on catching myself when I've created expectations. I remind myself that I'm likely to generate drama in my life, and then I focus on letting go of my expectations. My partnership is certainly a place for me to practice this on an ongoing basis.

It was Halloween weekend. My partner and I had just had some breakthroughs in spending time together and creating family (yes, after the camping adventures). I had asked him the previous week if he wanted to go out for Halloween, since it had been years since I'd enjoyed an adult Halloween celebration. I was excited about the thought of dressing up and going out on the town. He got weird about my question about going out together on Halloween, and sort of mumbled a vague and avoidant response. I've learned over time that this is often his way of saying, "No," for whatever reason.

Given his response, I was prepared to have a quiet and productive weekend at home. There were lots of chores, work items, and errands that I needed to catch up on. In fact, a quiet and productive weekend was probably exactly what I needed at the time to enhance my peace of mind.

That Saturday Halloween night, I was sitting at the kitchen table working on my laptop. The dishes were done, I had taken a shower, the candle was glowing on the kitchen counter, and the treats were sitting by the front door. I was ready, but 5 p.m. passed, and 5:30 p.m. passed, and 5:45 p.m. passed. No trick or treaters. My mind started racing, thinking that the last thing I wanted was to be at home alone on Halloween night, like completely alone without my kids and without trick or treaters.

My neighbors from across the street rang the doorbell with their two-year-old dressed as a bird. They invited me to walk around the block with them. I immediately declined, and then noted to myself that I would be choosing to bask in my loneliness, when I was actually upset about feeling lonely. I admitted to my neighbors that I only had three kids come to the door so far. They laughed, told me to leave a bucket of treats outside the door for kids to help themselves to, and come out with them. I agreed.

I really had to catch myself and identify my expectations before I got emotional. I had an expectation that because my partner and I had been spending more time together, and more time together as a family, that meant that we would be together that weekend, especially given that it was a holiday. I also had an expectation that he would at least text and check in with me that night. He had been at a conference that day, and had sent a picture from the event, but I didn't hear from him afterwards. I purposely didn't ask him what he was up to because I have a belief in giving space, and trusting that if he wants to check in and share what he is up to, he will.

I even caught myself beginning to formulate a story that sounded like: "Well, it has been nine months, and if he is just pretending that he wants family, but is really going to be in and out for the rest of our relationship, this isn't going to work. It's not acceptable for him to just disappear. Or, maybe I'll just get a roommate. Yes, a male roommate. Let's see how he likes that. If he's not going to be around, I'll find someone who is."

I had to play "devil's advocate" to move past my expectations. I asked myself, "What may he be thinking, or not thinking?" Then I continued the conversation with myself (come on, I know you talk to yourself too.) "First, he's not from Canada, so he may not even be aware of the cultural importance and emphasis on the celebration of Halloween. Second, he may just need a break from the time we've been spending together. After all, it's a transition. Third, maybe he doesn't like dressing up. Fourth, how can I expect him to know that I had been hoping to be together tonight, if I didn't communicate this with him?"

As I fell asleep that night, I focused on being grateful for the long and restful sleep ahead of me. I would wake up the next morning, without the ramifications of a few too many glasses of wine. I would be productive, and get a whole bunch of work done. I'd had a lovely time walking around with my neighbors.

Now, this doesn't mean that I wasn't disappointed, because I was. And it doesn't mean that I wasn't lonely, because I was. But what helped me to stay calm and grounded was recognizing that I myself, and my expectations, had put into motion the escalated emotions and dramatic stories. I'm always working on enhancing my ability to moderate my expectations, and to remain in power. We can turn our expectations from negatives to positives, quite quickly.

I learned through this example that it's best to give someone the benefit of the doubt (and judge someone favorably), than to suffer resentment that inevitably bleeds into the relationship. I learned to roll with the punches, make the best of the situation, instead of simmering over comparatively nothing – and wasting a lot of time doing it.

When were you disappointed and upset recently? In what ways can you see that you allowed your expectations to take you over?

_____

_____

_____

As I mentioned above, we can be proactive with our expectations by recognizing them early.

I recently found myself stewing about how I suspected that my partner would duck out of picking me up at the airport on my return home from a 10-day trip.

I was scheduled to arrive home at about 11 p.m. on a Saturday night. This scenario had happened before, and I caught myself playing the movie through in my mind: boy promises girl a pick-up at the airport; girl fantasizes about long, romantic kisses of reconnection at the airport; girl fixes her make-up upon landing and feels her heart pounding as she gets more and more excited to see boy; boy texts girl and asks her to take a cab because he's had a few too many beers. Wait... I'd seen that movie before, and I remember the girl was pretty darn cranky when she got out of the cab at home.

We can avoid disappointment and remain in power of ourselves by recognizing how we may be setting ourselves up for drama with our own expectations. As we were having our night cap of a glass of red wine one night, my partner asked, "When do you get home again? What time am I picking you up at the airport?" I reminded him that it was 11 p.m. He sighed and said, "Ugh. It's so late. And I'll probably be in the middle of a huge Nerf gun battle with the kids." I smiled and responded, "You know what, I'm not going to count on you picking me up at the airport. I'm going to be excited to see you, and I don't want to get upset if you decide not to come at the last minute. I'm just going to plan on taking a cab."

Now, I should say that these preventative measures work really well, except in cases when what you are hoping for, or expecting, is super important to you. We can get better at flowing naturally with how people and events and circumstances play out, but we do need to be mindful of when something is super important to us. In these cases, communicating and standing for what we want assertively is the best bet. Compromising and accommodating on these deal breaker needs will just result in us being surly, scrappy, and spiteful.

Do the Right Thing

We gain energy and power in life when we do the right thing, exceeding our own expectations. We become leaders and legends in our own minds, in a good way. This isn't about ego and looking good. When we know that no one is watching, or that no one is holding us accountable, or that no one is going to offer us any acknowledgment, it's an opportunity to do the right thing and to prove to ourselves that we have a deep commitment to maintaining our integrity, just for the sake of being internally powerful.

When I take an action (or don't take an action), I endeavor to do it with integrity and respect. For example, I put my trash in the garbage in the hotel room. And if it's a creamer and sugar package, I empty them into the sink first so that they don't spill into the unlined trash can that the cleaning staff will need to wipe. The first act of disposing of my garbage is integrity, and the second act of anticipating a mess is the respectful one. The act of emptying the contents of the creamer and sugar package into the sink takes all of two seconds of my time.

When I was walking my kids to school with a girlfriend recently, she said, "Oh I have something to tell you!" As she began to set the stage for an interaction that happened between her son and my son at school, I felt butterflies in my stomach, thinking that my son had been misbehaving.

She explained that her son, who is in the same grade but a different class as my son, had dropped a bunch of stuff from his backpack onto the floor in the hallway one day. My son apparently walked over and began helping him pick the items up. That night, my girlfriend's son reported to her what happened and said, "You know, Mom, he is a good friend. He did that without me even asking." My heart swelled as my girlfriend told me the story. I recognized that my kids have been learning the importance of doing the right thing, and are already starting to demonstrate doing the right thing in their own lives.

I believe that when we exercise our integrity, and help others, we choose to live powerfully.

Listen, be respectful, return borrowed items, follow the rules, clean up after yourself (or leave things better than you found them), cooperate, use your manners, don't bring peanuts in your lunch. In kindergarten, we have teachers and peers intently watching over us to make sure we do the right thing, yet later in life, we neglect to hold ourselves to the same standard.

For the most part, we know what the right thing to do is, but let's just take a bit of time to get reacquainted with what this can look like:

- At a restaurant, return the server's pen that you borrowed
- Say "please" when making a request
- Go back to a store if you were not charged for an item
- Push your chair back under the table
- If you call a taxi, be ready to go
- Pick up paper products off the floor of a public washroom
- Recycle

- Give compliments to people about their personality, quality of service, or appearance
- Refrain from wearing scents, especially if others have allergies
- Only take what you need from a buffet, a pile of items, etc.
- Pay money that you owe
- Clean the fridge in the staff room
- Mail someone a congratulations, get well, happy birthday, housewarming, or condolence card
- Dispose of your gum, cigarette butts, and any other litter
- Be gracious with caretakers such as nurses, teachers, babysitters, etc.
- Let others finish speaking
- Refrain from being cranky with telemarketers
- Be on time for appointments, or communicate as soon as possible if you anticipate being late

One "right thing" that I strongly believe in doing is to minimize my use of disposable containers and wrapping. I use my travel coffee mug every day, and I even have a reusable smoothie cup with a straw. The cashier and cook at the food booth where I often purchase Japanese teriyaki beef for lunch know that I bring my own ceramic plate with me, rather than accepting their white Styrofoam takeout container. If I'm at a restaurant and I can wrap my leftover burger or sandwich in a napkin, I do that rather than asking for a takeout container. (Some of my family members take plastic containers with them when eating out.) At a bakery, I'll say that I'm going to eat the bakery item right away, and that I don't need it in a brown bag. To live in a bubble and to ignore our place and impact in the world is a small way to live. There is always someone impacted by our action or lack of action. We have a duty to uphold our responsibilities, but I also think that if we are all going to work to turn the state of our world around, we also have a duty to go above and beyond.

Catch yourself thinking "too bad," or "it won't make a difference," or "I can do whatever I want," or "everyone does it," or "I'm just a small fish." We often tell ourselves some kind of story or make some sort of justification for not doing the right thing.

Instead, we can continually ask ourselves, "What's the right thing to do?" and "How can I go above and beyond what's expected?" and "How can I make this person's life easier?" I recently asked a girlfriend if she would mind picking up a box of my books at a store on her way to meet up for lunch. She graciously agreed. As she was packing them up before meeting me, she sent me a message and asked if I had a box to safely transport the books in. I said that I didn't, and she assured me she'd do her best to find a box of the right size and bring it with her. Now, not only did she fulfil on her word to pick up the books, she went above and beyond.

Imagine if all relationships and interactions in this world were "above and beyond" in nature! My aunt shared with me one day, "I have this dream that all of my relationships... well, everybody's relationships... would be extraordinarily generous. You know, a relationship where each person keeps giving to the other freely and lovingly. And each person is continually moved and impressed by the other's thoughtfulness. It's a constant, positive spiral of generosity and appreciation."

The right thing can depend on your values and perspective. Nonetheless, I challenge you to stretch your comfort zone to look past what you have traditionally thought is your responsibility, and to go above and beyond.

Where and how could do more of the right things?

_____

_____

_____

_____

_____

_____

I was at a large home store returning some sheets and three packages of shower hooks. When I looked down at my receipt after the transaction had been completed, I saw that I had been refunded nearly $300. I knew that the sheets were only worth about $50, and the shower hooks about $8 each. I said to the clerk, "Wait a minute. That seems like too much." I checked my receipt and noticed that she had mistakenly refunded me for a side table that I had not returned. She looked at me with a mix of surprise and relief, and exclaimed, "Oh, thank you! Most people wouldn't say anything. I'm so glad you did. I would have gotten in so much trouble. They may have even fired me!"

I'm far from perfect. I constantly need to check in with myself to hold myself accountable, and encourage myself to go above and beyond. I get caught up in the, "I don't wanna," conversation and the, "Well, no one else would go to that length," conversation. But I remind myself that it doesn't matter. It doesn't matter how I feel or what others are doing or not doing. Questions you could ask yourself to keep yourself grounded are:

- What might be the consequences of my actions? (in this case, a fired employee, or a stain on your conscience)

- What if everyone did it? (if everyone thought it was okay to litter, to not hold the door for someone, or to park over the parking lines)

- What if someone saw, who you didn't want to notice what you've done? (a priest/rabbi, your mother, your boss, your kids, a television crew)

Keep Your Word

There are likely people in your personal and professional life who you know you can count on. When they say they will do something, or be somewhere, you know that it's going to happen. They've shown you over time that they are someone who will follow through on their word. You probably love and respect them for their power and integrity.

I have learned that keeping your word isn't based on luck, and it's not a natural talent either; it is a powerful life skill that requires constant commitment and practice. Author of the bestselling *Seven Habits of Highly Effective People*, Stephen Covey, explains that as you break your word, you remove one grain of sand from your beach. It doesn't seem like a big deal at the time. But grain by grain, your beach gets thinner. Every time you go back on your word, you are reducing your own power.

As I have been developing my own skill of keeping my word, I have recognized that the first step is for me to be mindful and realistic about what I commit to. I don't say "yes" when I don't intend to deliver, or don't think it's realistic to deliver, or there are significant contributing factors out of my control. And I am getting much better at avoiding saying yes just to be polite. With my kids, I am mindful that it is tempting to respond, "tomorrow," to their requests, so I pay attention and try to explain if their request is a "maybe" – and even explain what factors or considerations delivering on their request hinges on.

I have learned to take stock throughout the day. I look at my to-do list throughout the day and consider the priorities in the context of what I have given my word to – what I have promised myself and what I have promised others. Especially in the evening, I look at what I gave my word to get done, and ensure I take care of everything I possibly can before going to bed.

If I have the energy to stay up and it's realistic to get a task done, I just get it done. If I absolutely don't have the time or energy, I put it at the top of my list for the next day. If someone else was counting on something from me, I let them know that I will do it tomorrow (specifically tomorrow morning if I see that I need to put it as my first priority in the day), or I give a specific, later date if need be.

My ultimate goal is to strengthen my skill of keeping my word so that it is solid gold – pure and powerful. A friend recently said to me, "I know you'll get it done Kara, because you said you'll get it done and you always do." Absolutely, this was flattering because it tells me that my peers are noticing that my commitment is a strong one. More importantly, though, especially over the last few years, I have been building trust within myself. As I discipline myself and practice this skill, I generate a high level of internal confidence that when I say something is going to happen, it happens.

Here is one example of building trust.

A colleague sent out an email to our national work team asking who would like to contribute to purchase flowers for a team member who was dealing with her mother passing away. Given the size of the group, I said that I would give $5, and that I would give the money to her when I saw her in a few weeks. When I got into town, I mentioned to another colleague that I needed to remember to give the $5. (Saying out loud what I need to do puts an anchor in my memory.) But, I saw my colleague twice over the next few days and forgot to give her the $5. Finally, I popped her an email saying that I'd give the money to her on Monday (the last day I would see her), and I placed a sticky note on my work cell phone to remind myself. It's only $5, but it is the principle of me fulfilling on my word that is critical.

I strongly believe that in order to strengthen our commitment to keep our word, we need to learn the impact that breaking our word has on others.

One interesting story is the time I was sitting in a parking lot at the airport, waiting to pick up my partner, so that we could go on a road trip to attend a family member's funeral. I couldn't pick up my partner, because he was with another person, who was waiting for a ride from someone who was an hour and a half late. The person who was late messaged my partner to say they were stuck on the snowy freeway.

I had just used the same freeway, and planned accordingly: I budgeted my time to ensure that if I was delayed, I'd still be on time.

Likely the other person in this scenario did not fully comprehend the impact of making another person wait. What resulted was that we drove in the middle of the night, through the snow, and arrived at our destination at 1:30 in the morning.

The thing is, unlike math and science, we are not taught how to recognize what impact breaking our word has on others. I now see that in past years I was quite oblivious to the impact that me breaking my word had on people. I didn't think about it. I just was living my life. I wouldn't consider the ripple effect of my lack of integrity.

Sometimes the impact is invisible, so we need to become more sensitive and better attuned to listen for, and see, our impact. For instance, on the road trip to the funeral, I updated my stepmother to say when we had reached our dinner break spot, but I didn't message her when we arrived at our destination at 1:30 a.m. I assumed they had gone to bed, but the right thing to do was to communicate. I found out the next day that she had stayed up worrying, and eventually gone to bed, but had a restless sleep. We always need to be looking to act with integrity.

On the whole, it's about being proactive and planning, gauging, and anticipating. We are talking about significantly enhancing chances of fulfilling your word, all the time. In the situation of the airport pickup, my partner could have explained to the other person the importance of her being on time, because of the drive and funeral ahead. The other person could have planned for a generous time buffer, knowing that winter roads in Alberta, Canada are unpredictable at the drop of a hat. (I, myself, had contemplated making two extra stops before heading out to the airport, but had decided not to so that I had plenty of time to get there on schedule.)

It doesn't work to make excuses, especially because we get better and better at making excuses and justifying our actions. We get into habits of logically and believably explaining what got in the way of us doing what we said we would. The other person doing the airport pickup may have thought, "I know I'm late, but it is understandable given the weather and road conditions. It's out of my control that the freeway is jammed. I even tried other routes. Besides, I was doing this pickup to oblige and to be nice – it wasn't even the original plan." I urge you, even if you contemplate committing to something to be nice, check in with yourself to make sure that you are 100% committed and prepared to make it happen before you give your word.

We also get in the habit of blaming other people. It's easy to look at the other person in a situation and to defer. We may say something like, "Well, he didn't give me what I needed, so I didn't get it done." But did you ask, remind him, or set up a plan? With the airport pick-up, I needed to admit to myself that I did not do my part, and make it clear how important it was to me that the timing of the pickup was executed extremely efficiently. With my stepmother and the road trip, I could say, "Well, she could have messaged me to ask where we were and request that I check in when we arrived." But should she have to do this? It's a practice and an art to hold ourselves accountable, and see what we did (or didn't do) to create us breaking our word, instead of pointing the finger at someone else.

To go one step further, I believe that we actually get good at attracting difficult circumstances to get ourselves out of keeping our word. Then we can legitimately say that we couldn't fulfil on our word for X, Y, and Z reasons that were out of our control. You may remember in *Chill* that I mentioned that one way to get things done in life is simply to give your word to it, and to say to others what you are committed to getting done. This is a powerful way to live, provided that you honor your word. That means that when you say something will get done, it gets done.

The foundation of honor and power is to keep your word for yourself, for your own integrity. This is a powerful and inspiring way to live, because you know that you can count on yourself, and others know that they can count on you.

Traci Costa...
on Be Powerful

"Human greatness does not lie in wealth or power, but in character and goodness. People are just people, and all people have faults and shortcomings, but all of us are born with a basic goodness."

ANNE FRANK

Traci is owner of Peekaboo Beans, a children's playwear company. When she became pregnant, she began shopping for her little angel Cailin – as a fashionista, this was top of her priority list. But Traci found as Cailin grew, that the clothes Traci purchased didn't wash well and weren't functional. After one or two washes, the clothing looked nothing like what it had on the rack when she bought it. Buttons and zippers and certain styles were awkward for her as a parent when dressing her wee one, but more concerning, they restricted Cailin's ability to move and play. Traci set out to design and produce a line of clothing that would last (for environmental reasons), and promote play (for developmental reasons).

I worked with Peekaboo Beans for a number of years, as one of the founding stylists promoting play and selling playwear under the company's direct sales platform. What drew me to Traci, the Peekaboo Beans team, and the mission of the company was that everyone and everything was rooted in strong beliefs of the value of family and children's development. Because of my passion for environmental preservation, I was particularly motivated to promote a product that would last and stay out of the landfill, given that "fast fashion" clothing has become one of the biggest contributors to worldwide waste.

Peekaboo Beans stands for a worldwide movement. Every year the company donates thousands of dollars to Playground Builders, a non-profit organization. Playground Builders uses the money to build basic playgrounds in developing countries. The founders of Playground Builders risk their lives to personally travel to these countries to negotiate and secure playground sites, and then coordinate the procurement of materials and the construction of the playgrounds. They have also created partners and volunteers over the years to assist with the process. By creating play in developing countries, they nurture children, the youngest and most innocent victims of war; in addition, Playground Builders strongly believes that playgrounds strengthen connection and community. In the end, transforming the social fabric of our developing communities by building playgrounds has the potential to mitigate or even prevent war.

~

Traci's dad is Japanese, and the youngest of six children. He was born during World War Two. His family's home was taken away, and they were shipped to internment camps in northern British Columbia, Canada. His brother and sisters were sent to different camps. Her dad was a baby at the time, and it was an extremely difficult experience for him to endure as a child. Her dad went back to Japan and then eventually returned to Canada as he grew up. But he was held back because he didn't have an education. Traci says he didn't have the basics of life that many of us take for granted, and essentially had to begin his life from scratch. Traci's mom, of English Danish descent, had her own challenges being born during the war. Growing up, she had a wonderful, committed family, but it was hard times. She was the eldest daughter of four girls (one severely handicapped), and had an alcoholic father. Traci's parents met in high school in the 60s, at a time when mixed race couples were a unique relationship.

Her parents' personal struggles and their marriage were difficult, Traci admits. She became a people pleaser, trying to control her parents' emotions and make them happy when they weren't. Their home wasn't happy, and her parents divorced when she was eight years old. She was uprooted to different schools and endured a lot of change through elementary school, so she entered high school with an unstable and fragile foundation. In high school, Traci was generally surrounded by people who were not "lifters."

"I ended up getting caught up in the gossip and the drama, and what high school brings. I did not stand for what my belief systems are, because I was afraid, and did not have the tools to defend my beliefs or myself."

She sees now that she was like a leaf in the wind – she moved up and down with the emotions of the people around her. "It was daunting because I didn't have a solid foundation." As she moved into her graduating years of high school, she did start to develop a stronger sense of herself and created some lifelong friendships and memories that have continued to be nurtured.

Traci recognizes that she brought her young life experiences and mindset into her marriage. She remembers being extremely defensive. For instance, her husband would ask in a casual tone, "Is there dinner tonight?" Traci remembers that she would immediately go into defending and explaining that she just got home from work. Rather than simply responding, she would internally defend herself and think, "You could cook dinner too, you know." She realizes now that she was making stories up in her head, and at a deeper level, was worried that she wasn't living up to her husband's expectations.

Sparked by years of infertility, Traci fell into a depression; she desired children so badly. Her friends were having babies, and everyone was going to baby showers. She became isolated because she didn't want to project her sadness onto others. She says there was an impact on her work and relationships – she didn't care, and she wasn't interested. It was a downward spiral. She would look in the mirror, and not even know who she was. She would just see sadness and loss.

Her doctor and her mother recommended that she seek professional help. Therapy helped Traci move through her depression. She started peeling back the layers, as she longed for happiness again.

"It was like undoing the pieces of the puzzle, to look at who I had become and why – and then reframing them, and putting them back together." Traci worked to shed the negative stories, and even shed friends who weren't serving her. She relearned who she is, and learned new tools.

Traci says that she had to work hard to create happiness. She wanted to be happy and to surround herself with happy people, and she wanted to be powerful, but she hadn't been set up for that.

"I needed to shed a lot of excess baggage."

Traci is thankful that her husband Brad came from a solid foundation. "Drama isn't in his nature," she explains, "And he taught me that life doesn't need to be that way."

Traci believes that we need challenges in life to make us reach for resiliency.

"I've learned through hard experiences, greatness can come. You certainly have to work at it. You have to work at being happy. You have to work at taking responsibility. And you need to reach out for support because doing it alone doesn't work. I worked so hard to feel comfortable, to feel whole – to be okay with not being perfect. I'm proud of this."

Through her growth, Traci came to a place of recognizing and accepting that her parents were dealing with their own challenges; for whatever reason, this was the way her life journey unfolded. She moved past being sad and angry. "It's not that I blame my parents for how I grew up. I just think that I built my life backwards. It's a different time now. Parents and children deal with different challenges as the times change."

Her husband Brad and she were successful in the process of in vitro fertilization. When she got pregnant, life looked completely different for Traci. Their first baby was born, and they named her Cailin.

The birth of Cailin sparked a deep passion within Traci – one that she believes was always there but had been squashed by her struggles in life. Cailin showed Traci that play is how children become who they are, and Traci began to rekindle her own playful memories. She had fond memories of spending time at her grandparents' cottage and could see how her attachments to her grandparents and play experiences had shaped her. She wanted to share this revelation on how critical play is for the health and well-being of children. She wanted to create a brand and a playful apparel product to spread this meaningful message.

Traci started Peekaboo Beans when Cailin was two years old. Her primary focus was to bring the right people into the company – positive, solution-focused, inspiring, creative people – and to create a strong culture. She has strived to get, and keep, the right people on the bus, so to speak. Even beyond creating a powerful product for a powerful reason, she wanted to create a powerful organization.

Through much coaching and personal development, Traci explains that she has learned leaders bring their unresolved issues into organizations, and then the organization lives them out. Traci has to be aware of what her issues are, and to continue to learn and grow, so that she doesn't live out her issues in the organization. She recognizes that everyone is raised under different roofs and with different values, so her intention has been to foster an accepting environment with emphasis on communication, and also with direction and aligned focus.

"I won't tolerate gossip, drama, and negativity because I came from that, and I worked so hard to change that. I'm all for communication and tough conversations, but I don't want to have endless conversations fraught with 'poor me' and 'life is against me' energy." She says at work, just as in any area of life, it's important to communicate in a productive and non-defensive way. Conflict inevitably arises, but you can have tough conversations and still come out of them ahead. In her own journey, she recognized how much of a people pleaser she had become, largely because of her childhood. She worked to become comfortable in the foundation of who she is, so that she could speak her truth and not always go with what other people say and do.

Traci is proud that Peekaboo Beans is a socially responsible company, and one that empowers thousands of women across the country to have choice and flexibility in their work, and earning additional income for their families doing what they love. The employees who work in the corporate office have significant leeway in the number of days and hours they work, plus time to look after family responsibilities. Women who sell Peekaboo Beans (via a direct sales platform) have complete control over their commitment level and hours. "It moves me to think about how many families we are touching, and how many women are building their lives on their own terms."

Traci's true passion is for play. "Having children, I realized that kids and their development is my deepest passion. I embrace who they are as people... and, see that they are all so innocent and full of life." Traci says that when you ask people to close their eyes and think of their fondest memory, most people think of a time when they were playing and felt free, happy, and inspired. Usually parents weren't around. There was pure enthusiasm, space, no rules, and freedom to experiment. Traci became enamored with children's love and need for play, and built Peekaboo Beans around her passion for fun and learning for kids.

She explains that despite how critical play is for children, it is becoming a lost art. Traci works with doctors and child development specialists, who are afraid of what is happening in the world.

"It is becoming a tiger parent world, where parents want their kids to be successful, and see play as frivolous. But the irony is that play is actually what makes kids successful. Play is how children communicate. Even more concerning is that there are children in the world who don't even have safe places to play."

Peekaboo Beans is more than a brand of clothing; the company stands for a movement to honor and protect children's need to play. Traci is proud of the profoundly touching "Play Revolution" video they created to send a strong message that play is essential for children. (The video is available to view on YouTube.)

Traci says that she doesn't focus on creating "balance" in life, because her work and family time is co-mingled – one blends into the other. "I've created a life where I can do both at the same time." Her girls have been involved in the business from the beginning, so that they have felt a part of it.

She admits that sometimes she feels conflicted, but most of the time she feels grateful that she can nurture her family and her professional life at the same time, and also offer the opportunity for her girls to learn in ways that they may not otherwise. "At the end of the day, I want them to be strong and independent, and make their own way. It's important to me that they see me doing that."

After ten years of infertility and multiple rounds of in vitro, Traci was blessed to conceive another miracle baby, Colbie, in 2008.

She didn't take a day off work during the pregnancy and after Colbie was born.

Colbie explains, "My mom goes to work every morning. I can phone her anytime I want, and I get to go to work with her all the time."

I asked Colbie what parts of being a part of her mom's work that she likes the best. "I like to spend time with my mom. At photo shoots, I get to spend time with my friends and we get to try on clothes. At meetings like this, I learn stuff about Peekaboo Beans."

Despite her passion for play, Traci admits that she hasn't had a full "fun" vacation in many years. She has tried to work less on vacation so that she is only working in the mornings and evenings.

"I don't have this mastered. It's still an area that I need to work on."

In addition to learning and growing through her challenges, and through founding and managing Peekaboo Beans, Traci is clear that her marriage has contributed to her expansion. "Brad and I have been together since we were 21, so from 21 to 47 we've gone through massive change, maturity, and growth."

Traci says that it sounds cliché, but communication is critical. Dialogue creates intimacy, flow, and pathways. She says sometimes she writes her husband letters and sends them to him. We need to be aware of the expectations we have with our spouse, she suggests. We need to communicate in a non-defensive and productive way. "You can have tough conversations and come out ahead."

It is key that each partner brings happiness into the relationship, she's discovered.

"The expectation that the other person is going to make you happy doesn't work. It's not about generating happiness from your spouse. You need to know what makes you happy so that you can keep creating your happiness, and when you both bring happiness, you can go on adventures together."

Fundamentally, Traci sees that the premise of a marriage is respect – respecting who the other person is, what his/her values are, and what makes him/her happy. "We need to preserve who we are, and also preserve who our partner is. It doesn't work to try to change the other person. A relationship is so much about understanding each other's path."

Traci doesn't try to hide the hard times. She talks to the girls and lets them know that the problems that mommy has are nothing for them to worry about, and that mommy will be fine, but to understand that life does have challenges. "I want them to know that you can jump over hurdles — and that sometimes you have to fall down in order to get back up."

She has worked to create strong attachments with her children, and she acknowledges that this had to come from a place of growth in herself, and power in herself.

"The challenges in life you face may be hard, but they'll shape who you are. Life isn't going to be full of rainbows and butterflies. If I hadn't gone through my journey with infertility, I wouldn't have started Peekaboo Beans." Finally, she emphasizes, "Believe in yourself. Have faith in yourself. Never hear, 'no,' as no. Never take setbacks as it's over. Listen to your inner voice. Trust your gut. Learn to trust your intuition."

Commit to Success

"Understand that the right to choose your own path is a sacred privilege. Use it. Dwell in possibility.'"

OPRAH WINFREY

At the end of the day, as I fall into bed, tapped physically and emotionally, if I can say that I gave my all and that I feel grounded, accomplished and connected, then it has been a successful day. The only thing that puts a cherry on top is a good orgasm.
There were times in my life when I went to bed at night wondering if the nightmare I was living in was going to end. I felt like I couldn't do anything right. I felt like I was never enough. I felt like I'd dug myself into a dark hole. The only thing that looked successful was what could be seen from the outside – where I lived, what I drove, and the certificates of accomplishment hanging on the wall.

To emerge from those times of darkness, it took me digging in to reconnect with what success means to me, and to take action after action that was uncomfortable, in order to get back on track. I had to trust that as long as I was clear about what my passions were, a higher power would carry me along a path of sharing my gifts with the world, and feeling the deep happiness that emerges from being on a journey of purpose.

I recommit to creating happiness and success on an ongoing basis, balancing the optimistic view that anything is possible, and the realistic view that some days and months are better than others. I don't think success looks and feels like unicorns and fairy dust every day. I can say that I've had a successful week or successful month or successful year if I have lived according to my definition of success.

For me, what creates success is doing what it takes to generate one successful day after another. The more days I go to bed feeling fulfilled, and the fewer days I go to bed feeling unsettled, I know that I'm headed in the right direction. The more days I go to bed feeling confident within me that I walked my talk, and was a strong role model for my kids and my clients that day, the more successful I judge myself to be. The more I believe that I made a positive difference that day, the better I sleep that night, and the more energy I wake up with the next day.

Ante Up

It's not luck or genetics or the perfect storm that unveils success. It's going to take you committing to success. Sometimes it will seem like it just falls from the sky into your lap. And sometimes it will seem that it takes absolutely every ounce of your strength, courage, and determination to create and enjoy a moment or day of success.

Extraordinary success requires us to first want it. There have been many times in my life where there hasn't really been anything inherently "wrong" or" "bad" or "horrible" about a situation, but I have chosen to let go, shift, or head in a new direction because I'm committed to extraordinary success in all areas of my life.

For example, I have been in relationships that were better than the last one, but still not what I was looking for in the way of extraordinary. Life being "okay" or "manageable" or "getting better" doesn't define the level of success I'm committed to creating in my life, so I chose to move on. The choice to change the status quo usually involves facing and dealing with some deep emotions – the fears that have brought me to that place, and the fears holding me back from moving on.

I recognize that something better may turn up right in front of my nose, and also understand that I may need to grow internally and/or take some tough actions to generate something better. Either way, I ante up and commit to creating extraordinary. Like the journey to organizing a room, closet or storage space, I think sometimes the journey to generate success needs to get messy first. We need to first make the decision to get started. Then, we need to confront the old ways, disorganization, and clutter. Even though we wish the mess would magically disappear, we need to get into action, dig in, and clean up.

I think that one of the biggest mistakes we make is expecting success to emerge in a big bang; we suppose that success will wash over us like a massive orgasm, and completely transform our life. Perhaps we expect success to look and feel like a downpour of never ending happiness – all of a sudden, we would achieve ultimate success, and our life would be perfect afterward. Even though we know that this isn't logical, maybe we have an unconscious expectation that success is going to hit us one day, and we'll live life happily ever after.

Commit to creating fulfilling and consistent success in your life, whatever that looks like for you, despite your circumstances. Now, notice that I didn't say, "...given your circumstances." Never take circumstances for granted. There are handicapped people who are Olympic athletes. Women who have been told they will not be able to have children have adopted, gotten pregnant through in vitro, or sometimes have miraculously become pregnant. Drug addicts become inspirational leaders. People move to other countries with nothing, and build legacies. Circumstances create barriers only in our minds, not in reality.

Success doesn't happen to us; we create it continuously. Rather than expecting success to transpire in a wondrous squirt, we need to ante up and commit to create extraordinary success, and keep committing to create extraordinary success, in little ways one day at a time. We need to be open to success magically popping up in front of our nose, and we also need to be fully prepared to deal with the hurdles and circumstances we encounter as part of the adventure of learning and growth. And then even as we hit success goal posts, we need to remember to ante up again, move the goal post, and keep dealing with hurdles and circumstances.

Discover a Blank Space

You get to choose what success is for you. Success isn't what your friends say it is. It isn't what the television and magazines say it is. And it probably isn't what you've always thought it is. Are you ready to embark on an adventure?

First, let me start with a disclaimer. This section may challenge or even confuse you. We are continually looking for quick fixes, and ideas and tools that we can quickly implement. Discovering a blank space – identifying and clearing hidden and latent, limiting beliefs – is counterintuitive.

Delve into this critical step. We all know that success isn't measured by the color or length or style of our hair, yet we sometimes spend more time and money finding the perfect hairstylist, and the perfect mix of streaks and layers, rather than confronting the current level of success in our life, and committing to enhancing it. It may be uncomfortable to acknowledge some personal truths, but I guarantee that it will be worth it. When we are caught in limiting beliefs, we are the only ones who can choose to clear our space. I believe that before we define success, we need to get out of the way what may be clouding our thinking.

I spoke with a woman who shared that she was re-evaluating her passions and purpose, because she was heading down a new and fresh path in her life. She shared that in the first few decades of her life, she focused on supporting her husband's career. I commented that this is a noble endeavor, and certainly an adventure of learning. We laughed in genuine appreciation of what it takes to nurture and encourage a man, as he builds his professional world, and provides for the family. I shared that I think as a society we have lost appreciation and respect for the supporting role that women play when they choose to support their man as the breadwinner. I congratulated her for her commitment.

My point is, many people make decisions based on societal trends and pressures (often unknowingly), but what is right for us and our families at a time in our life is just what is right for us and our families. We need to focus on our own values, personality, family, and intuition, as we imagine and pave our success path. This woman chose to nurture her husband and children for a period of time, and that is what fulfilling success looked like for her.

There are extraneous ideas in society and random thoughts in our heads that we need to identify, and clear, from our space, so that they are not influencing our success path. Some people would say, "You should be a good wife and mother, and stay home." Others would say, "You shouldn't feel like you have to stay home, just because you are a woman." You may say, "I should go work because I am educated," or "I should be making money and contributing to our family income," or "I should put my family first and be at home because that's what my mother did for me."

First, whatever ideas you have about what you "should" do to be successful, or what success "should" look like, it's time to put all of them aside. It doesn't matter what is glamourous, expected, achievable, profitable, normal or abnormal. It doesn't matter what's acceptable or unacceptable in society. It doesn't even matter what you've been telling yourself. Because it is so common for us to make choices based on what others are doing, what the research says we should be doing, what the people in our lives advise us to do, and what we think we should be doing, we need to continually identify and ignore the "shoulds."

What are you doing in life because you think you "should" in order to *look* successful?

_____

_____

_____

_____

_____

_____

What are you doing in life because you think you "should" in order to *feel* successful?

_____

_____

_____

_____

_____

_____

Next, challenge your own sense of what success could be for you. It might be fun and do-able to spend a few months, or a year, abroad as a family. Or what about becoming an Erin Brockovich-like lawyer? Or what about heading up the fundraising committee in your spiritual organization? Or what about learning about composting? Or what about becoming a competitive athlete? Or what about generating a million dollars to open a socially conscious business? Or what about volunteering to hold babies at the hospital? Or what about putting on some sexy lingerie and high heels for a fun and sexy date? Or what about learning reiki? Or what about knitting mittens for the homeless? The more we say, "That's not me," the more we place restrictions on what we allow ourselves to be capable of.

And finally, let go of any and all of your limiting ideas of the ways in which success can or can't unfold. If we believe that success has to be a huge accomplishment, then we miss opportunities to produce "small" but fruitful successes every day.

If we believe that we are only capable of generating small successes, then we put limitations on the magnitude of success that we could possibly create and enjoy. If we think that something couldn't possibly happen, the more we block the universe from delivering magic into our lives.

What limiting beliefs related to success and yourself, do you need to set aside?

_____

_____

_____

_____

_____

Despite what society and our peers say success looks like, despite who we think we are, despite how we expect success to unfold, we need to open up to success beyond our imaginations. Napoleon Hill talks at great length in his work about how some of the most "successful" people have been people who are not educated in the traditional school system. He also talks about how some of the most financially wealthy have been people who have experienced bankruptcy. Truly, our minds are the only constraints on our success possibilities.

Chica 90

The space of the future is unknown anyway, so I believe that I am much better off to step into a blank, boundless future space, than a cluttered and limiting space. The foundation of my success is to keep opening myself up completely to all possibilities. This blank space provides a true clearing for success to emerge in beautifully synchronistic and extraordinary ways.

Now Define Success

It doesn't matter what success looks like from the outside. We all know the feeling of success comes from within. There are people who look successful who aren't happy, and there are people who are happy but don't look successful. We need to stop looking outside of ourselves – comparing ourselves to others, and using external indicators – to demonstrate our success. We need to connect what makes us happy on the inside, to what it looks like on the outside through our definition of success.

I've heard countless women say over the years that they feel they are living in a fog. They are mentally and physically exhausted. One day blends into the next. Living an extraordinary life and being successful, in all areas of life, and in line with their passions and purpose, is beyond their imagination.

We work through a transformational exercise in my "Powerful Purpose and Passion" program where participants evaluate what areas of life they feel successful in, and what areas they do not feel successful in. Most people share insights along these lines:

• They have been striving to create "balance" in their lives because that is what everyone is talking about and says to do. They now realize that rather than aiming for "balance," they need to connect to their passions and mission, and focus on what success would look like in each area of life.

• Rather than feeling guilty that they are not doing enough, they need to start giving themselves credit for all the things they do already. They want to appreciate the success they have already created, and they know this will enhance their level of internal power.

• Everyone else appears so much happier in their lives, but it takes connecting with a group of people and having truly authentic dialogue to understand that most people are facing more challenges in their lives than they lead on. With reflection, action, and support, all of us can take small steps to heighten the level of success in our lives in big ways.

We need to create our own definition of success by our own passions, measure our own success by our own standards, and enjoy our own accomplishments by our own celebrations. Success is going to be what creates happiness in your heart, and only you truly know what brings forth that deep sense of fulfillment in you. It's what feels "right" for you. You will know the real reasons that you want to create success in a certain way. What others are doing, and what others think of what you are doing, is irrelevant.

Success is unique for each person. Success may look like getting fit, or volunteer coaching for a children's sports team, or inventing a piece of sports equipment. Success may look like starting a charity project, working in a charitable organization, or donating time or money to a charity. Success may look like renovating your kitchen to enjoy beautiful family meals, or building homes in developing countries, or offering handyman services to help handicapped and aging individuals outfit their homes.

Let's get a start on looking at what success really means to you. In the first column below, list 10 times in your life when you felt most successful. Place emphasis on the times when you truly felt a sense of inner accomplishment, rather than the times when you received external acknowledgment.

1. _____   _____

2. _____   _____

3. _____   _____

4. _____   _____

5. _____   _____

6. _____   _____

7. _____   _____

8. _____   _____

9. _____   _____

10. _____   _____

In the second column above, write down what made you feel successful. What are the common threads? What brings you feelings of joy and success? (For example, laughter, contribution, risk, nature, challenge, creativity, autonomy, adventure, health, peace, efficiency, companionship, beauty, innovation, etc.)

We need to look at what lights us up and makes us feel successful at our core, and then consider what success could look like in all areas of our life – health, family, professional, fun, spirituality, finances, community, etc. Success in each area is created through diligent and persistent action, and magical manifestation, in alignment with our unique and personal definition of success.

Just after my recent birthday, I was reflecting with gratitude about the success of the day, and the level of success I've worked to create in my life. My day looked like this: being a guest speaker in an online seminar; making a beautiful breakfast (omelette, hash browns and fruit) with my partner; driving across the city to pick up my daughter at dance; running an errand; doing some writing; powering through a workout; watching my son's soccer game; and enjoying the wine, balloons, and cake that were thoughtfully prepared at home.

Because my day reflected what I deem as success in a number of priority areas in my life, it was the perfect day. Friends and family members kept asking what I was doing that was "special" that day, especially after I shared that I had been taxiing kids around. But I didn't feel that I needed unicorns or fairy dust. I was happy. It was a steady, fulfilling, and extraordinary day.

Once you become more grounded in what creates that inner sense of warmth and accomplishment within you, you will become far less concerned with: the traditional and external measures of success; what others seem to think and say you should do to be successful; and the extent to which you are suitable or capable of achieving success. You will quiet your internal dialogue – your doubting, worrying, and questioning – that takes you away from actually enjoying the success that you are already achieving in your life every day.

You will be clear and confident in what success means to you, and in full control of generating success one day at a time. Even on a bad day, you can remind yourself that this is what fulfills you on a deep level. As you feel more and more of that inner sense of warmth and accomplishment, you will be even more open and curious to explore what would take your life to that next higher level of success.

Success is going to be what creates happiness in your heart, and only you truly know what brings forth that deep sense of fulfillment in you. It's what feels "right" for you. You will know the real reasons that you want to create success in a certain way. What others are doing, and what others think of what you are doing, is irrelevant.

What could extraordinary success look like in your health?

_____

_____

_____

What could extraordinary success look like in your family?

_____

_____

_____

What could extraordinary professional success look like for you?

_____

_____

_____

What could extraordinary success look like for you in creating fun and adventure?

_____

_____

_____

What could extraordinary success look like in the area of
_____?

(Choose a priority area of life for you – such as spirituality, finances, sexuality, community, friendships, etc.)

_____

_____

_____

Do What's Uncomfortable

Success can be easy, but it's not always easy. At times, success emerges beautifully, naturally, and peacefully. At other times, it starts out messy. We may need to take actions that are gruelling or tedious. Creating success isn't always comfortable.

My cousin recently shared with me, quite humbly and candidly, that he finds himself wanting to take it easy, be lazy, and not dig into tasks that he knows would contribute to him moving forward. He said that one day blends into the next and it's easy for him to say to himself, "Oh, maybe tomorrow." He admitted that even though it is so simple, really the only remedy to this pattern and way of life is for him to stop letting the "I don't wanna," internal dialogue get in the way of doing what would be beneficial. Here are my thoughts:

• Context: The more I get clear on what success means to me in the way of nurturing myself and my family, and making a difference in the world, the more willing I am to get done what needs to get done (regardless of how I feel), in order to take on bigger challenges. The little, mundane "I don't wanna" tasks seem less significant in the face of my commitment to make a difference on this planet. I don't have the time or energy to complain about, procrastinate on, or even perfect tasks because I know I have other important work to do. And as I simply take care of the little, mundane tasks that "I don't wanna" do, I have more time and energy to continue taking on bigger challenges.

• Diligence: Many times there is just no way around that a commitment requires hard work and sacrifice. There have been many, many days, nights, and weekends, when I have chosen to work rather than going to dinner, to the movies, concerts, local events, etc. Rather than shopping, having coffee with a friend, playing video games, or going to the spa, I have been attending workshops and volunteering at seminars in order to learn and grow.

• Expansion: As I take on bigger and bigger commitments on tighter and tighter timelines, I have to push myself to overcome fear and self-doubt; I have to push myself to further develop my efficiency, self-confidence, creativity, communication, and intellect beyond what I think I am capable of. Just as I experienced an adrenaline rush when I went skydiving, I experience an adrenaline rush when I am planning my daughter's birthday party the day before her big day because I have been spending my time coaching clients. I experience an adrenaline rush when I am meeting a prominent philanthropist for the first time, but I haven't had time to do my make-up because I've been making my kids' lunches and dropping them off at school.

One particular opportunity ended up being a chance to do something uncomfortable – and extremely rewarding. I decided to purchase a piece of land in Costa Rica, and did so because Teresa de Grosbois and Pam Bayne, leaders of the Evolutionary Business Council, were committed to bringing together a group of thought leaders and to create a sustainable retreat community. The financial commitment was out of my comfort zone, and a number of caring friends shared with me their concerns about the risks of the purchase, but I was up for embarking on an adventure to make it happen.

After I committed to the purchase, my priority was to earn and save money in order to fulfill the requirements of the payment schedule. Every day and every week, I looked at how I could earn, recuperate, and save money. I sold items that we didn't need through the online classifieds, $5 at a time. I resisted buying a new laptop even though friends made fun of my ancient laptop. I used coupons when treating the kids to a dinner out.

I'm not going to lie: from start to finish, gathering the money to buy the land in Costa Rica was truly an adventure. In a plight to secure a Home Equity Line of Credit in order to make one of my payments, I had to deal with two different bankers in order to get the approval I needed. When it looked like the first banker wasn't going to get the approval through on time, I sought out a different banker. A few months later, when I was setting up my final international wire payment at the bank, the teller informed me that, even with the overdraft on my account, I was short money. I asked her how much I was short. When she informed me that it was about $60, I looked down at my phone, remembering that I had just received an email money transfer for about $63 a few hours earlier. I deposited the email money transfer into my account, and the teller sent the wire.

Despite the fear and anxiety that I felt, and despite the measures required to create the funds for the land in Costa Rica, my intuition said that it was the right thing to do. I was fully aware that it was the biggest and riskiest financial decision that I had ever made. I was aware that as a self-employed, single mom, this was not exactly a decision that most would make. Yet, Costa Rica aligned with my passion for creating a sacred retreat space for my training sessions. And the money for my payments seemed to arrive in my account just in time, many times within 10 dollars of what I needed, throughout the process.

Once the land was paid for and I needed to travel to Costa Rica to complete the legal paperwork, it wasn't comfortable for me to think about making the trip. I tried a few times to talk my partner into coming with me, but he declined. It's not that I haven't travelled or travelled on my own – I had backpacked through Southeast Asia with my parents as a teen, lived in France in university on my own, and visited my mom when she lived in Abu Dhabi. But I'd never been to South America, and knew that the travel wouldn't be like taking an all-inclusive trip to Mexico. Thankfully, my mom offered at the last minute to come with me, but because our flights were a day apart each way, I'd still be breaking ground on my own.

On my arrival, the adventure began in full force. I was unable to get a chip installed on my phone in order to get cell coverage because my phone was locked. As I walked out of the San José terminal late in the evening, I was bombarded by men asking me where I was going, trying to talk me into taking a taxi or renting a car with them.

At the car rental office, they disagreed with me that my credit card covered the insurance they were trying to sell me (my friend Tina Dietz had warned me that they'd push to sell me insurance), so we waited on hold with the credit card company for about 45 minutes to verify the coverage. At this point, I realized that I was actually at the wrong car rental company office, so I walked back across the road to the airport terminal, requested that security allow me back into the terminal where the car rental booths were located, and had the correct rental company give me a lift to their office about five minutes away, putting me there at about 10:30 p.m.

An hour later, I was driving through the dark, deserted, unmarked back roads of San José searching for my three star hotel, looking in the rear view mirror to make sure I wasn't being followed. I was grateful that the gentlemen at the car rental office had insisted that I purchase a GPS with my rental, once I had admitted I had no cell coverage.

Throughout our four concentrated and focused days, my mom and I adventured in: getting Spanish navigational directions, navigating the unmarked town streets, walking through the jungle-like property with the developers, meeting with home builders, signing documents with the lawyer, visiting local markets and cafés, having cold showers at the bed and breakfast, and taking taxis into town at night.

And, the end of the trip brought forth the grand finale. My mom and I had decided we wanted to drive to the beach on our last day of this trip, so I had spent the day driving on the mountains – careening through hairpin turns and hugging the shoulders with steep cliffs below. When we made our way back to San José that afternoon, we checked my mom into her hotel (as she was flying out the next morning). Then we filled the car with gas, and drove the route to the car rental office, so that I was set up to return the car and get to the airport on my own that night.

A few hours later, as I drove down the road toward the car rental office, I heard a gunshot and saw police lights flashing in the gas station adjacent to the car rental's parking lot. I quickly scanned my surroundings and focused on pulling into the lot. As the guard raised the arm for me to drive into the lot, a few of the rental agents were running out of the office, across the parking lot, and were motioning for me to stay in the car. I sat in the driver's seat half ducking, and half scanning the lot, to assess the situation, and play out possible scenarios with plans of action. After a few minutes, the rental agents came walking back across the lot, and motioned for me to come into the office. "How was your trip?!" they asked me. "Oh...interesting!" I responded.

As I said, the Costa Rica extravaganza has pushed me out of my comfort zone in many ways already, and I expect that I will keep being pushed, as I continue travelling there and pursue building there. I know though that the experience is unfolding with flow, in alignment with my passions and intention. The journey won't necessarily be peaceful, but I'm up for riding the flow and I'm willing to do what's required.

I believe that we need to create a definition of success, and commit to creating success, in a way that ignites extreme passion, charge, and even urgency. We need to create a powerful context. If someone granted you with the responsibility of rescuing a drowning child from the river, the "I don't wanna" swim in cold water conversation would be irrelevant in the context of saving a life. Similarly, your definition of success needs to powerfully call to you.

We also need to dig in and do things we "don't wanna" do in order to create a higher level of success. It's just the way it is. We need to have an uncomfortable conversation with someone. We need to clean up a mess (a physical mess or an emotional mess) that we've made. We need to move or start a new job or release weight. We need to make a tough decision that may upset others. We need to take accountability for a mistake we've made. We all know that some of the most important decisions we make and actions we take are uncomfortable. On an ongoing basis, we need to look at what we need to do rather than what we want to do. Nike says it best: "Just Do It!"

And finally, we need to embrace expansion by stretching our comfort zones to take on a project or task, and dive into uncomfortable action, so that the level of challenge creates an experience of adventure. If we find ourselves dwelling and daydreaming in the "I don't wanna" conversation, it's a sign for us to kick ourselves in the butt.

Trust the Flow

When I am in flow, success often comes to me. Like attracts like, so when I am feeling grounded, productive, and focused on tasks that align with my passions and purpose, I am pleasantly surprised with how easily I generate success. When I find myself pushing hard to get something done, I stop and remind myself that I'm committed to creating a life of flow. As I embrace more and more flow into my life, and details work out, this leaves me considerably more time and energy to devote to the projects that I've identified will make a difference in the world.

Ease shows up in many little ways. For instance, there was a time I took donuts to the car dealership where I had purchased a vehicle, where I received tremendous service from four associates working in collaboration. I needed to do three things: give the donuts, have a protective coating installed on my windshield, and pick up a bonus gift card that I had been promised as part of the deal. I presented the donuts to the sales manager, who immediately shared them with one of the salespeople. About 15 minutes later, as I was sitting in the waiting room working on my laptop and waiting for the coating installment, the associate who had assisted me with the financing process approached me to present the gift card. He said that he'd just been in the sales manager's office eating a donut, and discovered that I had brought the donuts in. See, I didn't need to seek him out to pick up the card. He came to me. This is just a small example of how when I let go, take genuine and generous actions, a number of the details of life (small and big) simply work out without me attending to them.

I am strengthening my ability to acknowledge when I am feeling impatient and anxious that life isn't unfolding in the time and process that I think it should. At these times, I am usually pushing, working hard, and bumping into challenge after challenge. I remind myself to trust the natural order of events and timing. I am getting better at catching myself analysing, planning, and worrying. I remind myself to slow down my internal dialogue, tap into my intuition, and take action one step at a time.

I also catch myself feeling anxious when life is flowing smoothly. I have found at various points in my life, when I was creating one success after another, I started wondering when life was going to go sideways. In a conversation with one of my coaches, Tracy Blehm, I admitted that I'd been on a roll with my goal reaching. At the same time, I found myself confronted with a worry of the success disappearing. She supported me in self-reflecting, and I began to recognize a hidden and limiting belief: that I thought it wasn't possible to achieve results and success as easily as I was.

I saw that if I continued to wait and expect for life to go sideways, I would probably see challenges. The path of self-limitation and self-sabotage was right there waiting for me if I chose to take it. But I was committed to growing and learning through this. As MarBeth Dunn, host of TheHavingItALLShow, says, "You attract miracles by releasing your belief that you don't deserve them."

My belief is that life, on the whole, doesn't have to feel gruelling and hard. Even when we are in flow, as we stream over rocks, and waterfall down cliffs, it may feel hard at times because persistent and/or difficult action is required. But on the whole, we need to commit to moving in a purposeful and meaningful direction. The more we define what success is to us according to our mission and passions, the more we will be called to carve our path.

Overcome Fear of Success

It is critical to consider what it takes to overcome the fear of success. We begin to see that our fears are embedded in stories that have been inherited or manufactured. The stories are not true. They are just stories. In fact, we can re-write our own stories. We often have a host of hidden, negative beliefs that subconsciously create fear of success, and thus limit our success. These are not easy fears to admit. But just by admitting them, we begin to face them. For instance, we may think that we shouldn't be more successful than our parents or siblings. Or perhaps there is an underlying stinginess and reluctance to share wealth produced from our successes.

As I have been reflecting with my coach about my fears of success, I have come up with the following:

- Losing touch with friends

- Running into harsh critics of me and my work

- Becoming irresponsible with wealth

- Becoming egoistic from success

- Experiencing a negative effect on the relationship with my partner

- Having to work harder to earn and deserve the success

- Having to prove my intelligence by completing more education, such as a PhD

- Dealing with others seeking my wealth (subconsciously and consciously) due to greed

- Being judged by my family and friends (due to their jealousy)

- Losing my privacy in the community, on social media, etc.

- Being recognized as a leader and role model, and then making a mistake

What do you think successful people need to do or be that you're not willing to do or be? What do you think successful people need to deal with that you don't want to deal with? What mistakes have you seen successful people make that you don't want to make? Don't judge or evaluate the fears that intuitively arise for you. Just write them down.

Take time for this next exercise. You may want to work on this exercise a few times over the next number of days. Honest responses will require some deep self-inquiry.

What are your fears?

_____

_____

_____

_____

_____

_____

One of the fears of success that I am working on is accepting that others will judge me and my success. At first I wrote that I am working on "dealing with others' judgments of my success," but there really isn't anything to deal with. I need to constantly remind myself that I have no control over what others think, and that their perceptions and judgments are based on their own experiences, limiting beliefs, and criticisms of themselves. This isn't a model, theory, or skill to learn, it is simply a commitment to an ongoing practice of noticing my fear of others' judgments, reminding myself that it's something I have no control over, and letting go. I find that the best way to let go is to get into action in order to move my mind from daydreaming to being productive.

I have been annoyed and disappointed with what people have said about some of my colleagues and their successes. For instance, people have attributed my colleagues' success to schmoozing with the right people, or sacrificing their integrity, or picking only the easy and lucrative work. Yet, I have worked closely with these same colleagues on a number of projects and experienced them to be the most diligent, gracious, organized, generous, creative and ambitious people that I know. My experience in working with these colleagues illustrates to me the reasons why they have created success in their lives.

When I find myself judging people for judging my colleagues negatively, I stop myself, because me being judgmental about others being judgmental only results in me being a hypocrite! I remind myself that we will all judge, and even though I have a commitment to catch myself judging, other people will continue to judge. It is what it is.

As I place less and less importance on the opinions and validations of others, those who choose to see me in a negative light naturally fall away in perfect flow. Instead, I focus on my passions, and my intentions for making a difference in this world, because I believe that making a positive difference is what creates value, which is what generates emotional and financial abundance. Every day, as I continue to journey on this process of living my purpose, some people fall away by their own choice. I choose to fall away from others by my choice. This blank space makes room for new friends – comrades and champions – to emerge, and we are naturally compelled to inspire and encourage each other because of who we are and what we are committed to in life.

Our fears of success create gusty winds that blow out the flames of success we ignite, so we must actively identify and work through them on an ongoing basis to ensure that we shine our lights bright in this world.

Let Go of Knowing

Anything is possible, yet we pretend to know what is possible for us. We say we are too old or too young. We say we are not smart enough. We say we don't have time. We say we don't have the money. We say we're not that kind of person. When we put these words out into the universe, we are saying that we already have it figured out what is possible based on who we think we are, and the circumstances we see that we have. But, we are denying the universe the opportunity to produce miracles beyond our imaginations. We are putting a cap on our success possibilities.

Never say, "never". Are you open to considering that you can dissolve all the notions of who you know yourself to be? We have so many preconceived ideas and stories about who we think we are and what we think we are capable of, which creates a comfort zone so much smaller than our actual potential. We think we know ourselves, yet we have the divine capacity to continually evolve and to transform.

My commitment is to continue acknowledging and setting aside my own notions of who I think I am, who I think I can be, who I think I should be, and who I think others expect me to be. Instead, I focus on who I need to be in the moment. A situation may require me to be courageous, resourceful, vulnerable, or something else at a level I never thought I was capable of. When I dig deep and step up to the plate to stretch as a person, I create internal success. I prove to myself that I am always capable of being someone beyond who I already know myself as.

Continually remind yourself to let go of trying to figure out how the future is going to unfold. Rather than being fixated on having a process figured out in advance, and being attached to how it's going to go, spend more time thinking about one step at a time and what your next logical and do-able action step is based on the current circumstances.

Especially when I catch myself analysing and postulating, I affirm to myself that I am living in an ever-dynamic world. I can make decisions and take action to the best of my knowledge and abilities; I remind myself that there is never a perfect path or process. Rather than hypothesizing about how a variety of scenarios could play out, I affirm that I can't control others' behavior and consider who I need to be now in order to be powerful. Rather than focusing on how others have handled similar situations or circumstances, I reflect on my own values and intuition to determine which path and choices are right for me. Rather than seeking experts to advise me on the "right" decisions, I seek information, weigh and strengthen my options, and seek out coaching to support me in sorting through both the emotional and logistical elements of moving forward.

When you let go of who you think you are and how you think life could or should go, and focus more on creating extraordinary success in your life, opportunities and results unfold in unexpected ways. When you prove to yourself that you're committed to be and do what it takes to create extraordinary success, even when it's uncomfortable, and in spite of circumstances, who you know yourself to be expands, and what you think is possible in life expands.

One day at a time, focus on knowing this: you deserve success, and you are capable of generating it. Continually commit to yourself to create extraordinary success. There will be times when it will take everything within you to remind yourself that you deserve something extraordinary and that you have the power to create it.

Sarah Chan on...
Commit to Success

 "To do more for the world than the world does for you, that is success."

HENRY FORD

One of the reasons I chose to interview Sarah Chan is that she is a true leader in social and community issues in our city.

"My father lived in poverty growing up, and he immigrated to Canada with a one-way ticket and only $300. I was raised to believe that if you work hard, you can have anything. But, we are wrongly taught that people who can't provide for themselves are lazy. I've learned through my work that a lot of people living in poverty are some of the hardest-working people I've ever met. Poverty is so complicated," explains Sarah.

~

Sarah grew up in a typical Chinese, patriarchal family with her mom and dad (who are still married), older brother (who is two years older), and younger sister (who is six years younger). Her parents immigrated to Canada separately for their post-secondary education and met through school friends. They married in Canada, and decided to stay.

Sarah's parents were entrepreneurial and owned a number of businesses, so their family didn't operate on a 9-5 schedule. "As early as I can remember, my brother and I have been taking care of ourselves," Sarah shares. "Our parents clearly cared for us, and gave all of the comforts that any family could wish to have. Our parents worked really, really hard, and my brother and I fended for ourselves."

She was task-oriented, even at that time – helping with everything from laundry to dusting to invoicing, ever since she knew the alphabet. She didn't receive much positive feedback for tasks she did well, but she would receive negative feedback for tasks she didn't do well. So, she would be proactive and do a lot of tasks. She admits that she is more of a people-pleaser than her brother, so she would always be looking for ways to contribute and make her parents happy.

When her sister was born, Sarah began to raise her. "Everyone thought I was a teenage mom," she laughs. Anywhere Sarah wanted to go, she had to take her sister, or Sarah wasn't allowed to go. "I put her on the back of my bike when she was old enough, and I used to ride around with her on the rear rack. Since it was the 80s, we didn't have helmets. I used to pick her up from school. I used to take her out on the weekends to hang out with my friends."

"In a way, I feel sorry for her. I wasn't very gracious toward her. I think I had a lot of resentment for the responsibility."

Sarah used to have a big chip on her shoulder for how she grew up, but she now realizes that it was a gift. She used to be resentful that she did more than her brother, and that not a lot of appreciation was shown. She sees now that she learned how to carry on with life, even with complications. She learned how to take care of herself, and to do her activities, even with a child in tow. She learned how to be a very capable person, because of all of the responsibilities she was given. She learned that regardless of others' choices and behaviors, you still need to do what needs to be done.

Her mom and dad's view of success was to work hard to be successful, and it was particularly important to her dad to have things as evidence of their success. Her mom grew up in an affluent family, and her dad grew up in a poor family. They had a large house and lots of things. Sarah would clean the house every week, and it became clear that the more things you have, the more work it is, and the more time it takes. She says that having more things means that you have more things to clean, organize, reorganize, and distribute.

Today, she believes it is most important to focus on what brings you joy in life, rather than striving to "have it all", and expecting that things will bring you joy. She says the phrase "having it all" doesn't resonate with her. As such, she likes to shop at second-hand stores, and likes fine beauty, and things that have a story.

The focus for Sarah is more on having things that fulfill a purpose, rather than collecting things to demonstrate success.

"I strive to be practical about my choices. So my things need to have a purpose, and I don't like duplicating things. If I already have something that serves a certain purpose, I don't want another." Sarah's husband is the mayor of the city. Meanwhile, she teaches piano in their home and works with a number of community organizations. So, in their activities and in the events they attend, they encounter lots of swag. Sarah says if it's a canvas shopping bag, she'll probably take it, because it has a purpose and she'll use it. But if it's a t-shirt that won't be worn in their family, she'd rather the t-shirt go to someone who doesn't have a t-shirt.

"I have broad visions of what I would define as success. But most importantly, if my family is successful, I am successful. And vice versa – if I am successful, my family is successful."

When making a decision, she weighs considerations such as: how much time it's going to take, how much she can do on her own, how much help she will need, how long it will take, how much will it cost, how nice it needs to look. However, she's discovered that even if we set out on the wrong course, we can adapt.

This principle of adaptation is one of the keys to success, she believes. "I don't think it matters whether you're a new mom, or an old mom, or even a mom at all. I think being able to adapt to circumstances, and to environments, and to other people around you is key to being able to move forward and reach your goals. And that's not just about parenting; that's about everything."

One example of adapting is arranging schedules that enable efficient work.

Sarah's kids stay overnight every weekend with her parents so that she and her husband are available to work. Without her parents, Sarah says that they couldn't do the community service in the same capacity. Given that Sarah is self-employed, she didn't take a maternity leave, so her parents have always been a key part of her team.

Efficiency is a key success principle for Sarah. She sees that growing up she was pre-trained to do a lot of things all at the same time. Sarah says that the more efficiency she has in her life, the more resources (time and money) that she has to do what brings her joy. For instance, when she is shopping, it is usually to purchase an item to fulfill a purpose, such as snow pants that fit.

That concern for efficiency spills into her social justice. She is troubled by the amount that goes to waste in society. She attends a lot of events, and sees a lot of waste. Often at galas, black tie dinners, and other events, she will seek out the banquet manager to find out where the leftover food goes. She was recently at an event where she and another lady were joking about taking home the turkey carcass for soup. Sarah called the other gal on her bluff and they ended up sneaking into the kitchen, snagging some Ziploc bags, and packing up the turkey carcasses from the event. They tucked their turkeys under the table to take home. On other occasions, Sarah has taken home lobster heads from catered dinners to make broth for soup.

"It's really exciting to be in a position to influence – in my own tiny, small, minuscule way – big changes. I'm motivated by a culture change and I'm willing to wait 20 years plus because that's how long it's going to take for it to happen – it's going to take over a generation, if not more."

Sarah believes that making a difference is about creating a team and a movement, and sticking to it. "If you can articulate yourself, you can get people to join."

When her husband ran for mayor, they faced criticism and naysayers, but they were undeterred. Embarking on the campaign wasn't even their idea to begin with. But since their involvement in the city has always been at a grass roots and community level, the team around them saw their potential to make a difference. "So many people told us we were crazy – too young, too inexperienced. They said, 'You have to wait your turn,' and 'You don't know what you're talking about. That's just not how things work.' But if social change can't happen in one of the most prosperous places on Earth, where can it happen?"

We can change our own thoughts about ourselves, she maintains. We can rethink some decisions.

"We can't be anchored and held back by our own insecurities and our perceptions of what other people think about us. And, it's not healthy to think of ourselves all the time anyway." Sarah says that it's important to be self-aware and self-reflective, but not self-indulgent.

At the end of the day, Sarah believes that success entails her family and community thriving. Life, she has learned, is all about creating joy according to your personal priorities. "Be motivated by something that you really believe in – something outside yourself."

Create Magic

When you are open to, and believe in magic, and when you are willing to take action to create it, magic will unfold. It can seem that certain people routinely attract magic into their lives. Maybe they are lucky? Maybe they are smarter? Maybe they are destined? Creating magic is a choice and a commitment. Everyone deserves it and can create it.

We can look at how things are, and struggle to believe that at this time and place in our lives magic is just not going to happen. We can think that we just aren't "special" enough or deserving of magic. I truly believe that only our own minds create these limits.

Even though it's common to blame other people and circumstances for standing in the way of our magic, we, ourselves, are actually standing in our own way. Our lack of belief in magic inhibits us from attracting and embracing magic.

The point is, regardless of your past experiences, current views, and circumstances, a magical and extraordinary life is entirely possible – and probable if you're open to believing it and to creating it. Are you ready to create magic now?

Look in Front of You

Sometimes magic is right in front of our noses and at our fingertips. We may daydream about what it is we think would make us happy, and get caught up in thinking about how and why life would be better. We may watch other people and wish we had what they have. We can be so busy wishing for the perfect scenario when elements of what we want – or in fact exactly what we want – are right in front of us.

In university, I began to develop a crush on my girlfriend's best friend. We decided to embark on a road trip to the Calgary Stampede, a world renowned rodeo, with two of her guy friends from high school, one of them being her best friend. I was so excited that we were going to the rodeo with real cowboys (yes, they had tight jeans, cowboy hats, and big belt buckles) in a real, farm pick-up truck. We had a blast chatting, laughing, dancing, and partying.

After the weekend, I brought up with my girlfriend that I thought her best friend was very sweet and fun and asked, "Would it be okay if I asked him out?" Immediately, I could see emotion arise in her – what appeared to be jealousy or anger. I was surprised given that I had asked her a number of times if the two of them had romantic feelings for one another and she had denied it repeatedly. "I tell him everything, and he knows everything about me, but no, it's not like that," she had explained to me. She said that she would speak with her friend and get back to me.

A few long days passed with no report back. I was starting to become anxious, getting insecure that maybe he wasn't interested in me. I decided not to push the issue and trust that in time I'd either hear some good news, or accept that no news was a "no" for whatever reason. A few weeks later, my girlfriend told me that the two of them had done a lot of talking, and that my interest in her best friend had made them realize the level to which they cared for each other. They had officially become a couple, and their relationship was going really well. Even though they had each dated other people through high school, a beautiful partnership was right in front of their noses. A few years later, they married and they are together to this day.

Another perfect example of seizing a magic opportunity came with Denis Cauvier, an international author and speaker, who shared with me a story about the time he was in Memphis, Tennessee, trying to figure out how he would get some media exposure for his visit. As he was standing in the elevator at the Peabody Hotel, he looked up and saw daytime talk show host Phil Donahue walk in.

Given that Phil was there for the funeral of his father-in-law, Danny Thomas, Denis didn't think the time was right to approach him. Later on that night, Denis was second-guessing himself for passing up the opportunity, so he decided to go for a workout at the gym and hit the sauna to sweat off his moping. In the gym, right in front of him, he met a publicist, who ended up being a tremendous help in promoting Denis' book. This teaches us that it's important to keep our antennae up, because you never know what kind of magic is there just waiting for you to grab.

I mentioned in the first chapter of *Chill* that I was looking at returning to work with the government. The first government department that I had worked for in my career had indicated they would create a half-time position for me. I was excited that this would fulfill my need for financial stability, supporting me to pursue my passion for writing.

Unfortunately, that proved to be a prolonged and frustrating process, ending with no results. At first, I was told that paperwork needed to be done to create the half-time position. A few months later, I was asked to submit paperwork for my security clearance to be updated. A number of months after waiting for the security clearance to be processed, I was informed that the manager, a long-time colleague and friend who I was looking forward to working with, was retiring. A couple more months passed before the new manager contacted me to ask where we were at in the paperwork process, and if I was still interested in the position. Finally, weeks later, the new manager informed me that senior management had decided to shift the budget and they no longer had funds for the position.

At that point, I contacted human resources in the government department that I had last worked for – my "home" department. I had been in contact with them over the months to indicate my intention of returning to work with the other department. Now, I updated them on the situation, and explained that I had been promised a position, had been waiting eight to nine months to go back to work, and had now been informed that there was no longer funding for the position. I was more than ready to return to work and was wondering what my options were with my home department. After some quick research in the system, the HR consultant informed me that the position I formerly held was in fact still "mine" since the person who had been brought on to fill the position in my absence was on contract.

There are times when the magic you seek simply requires you to do a little legwork to harness it. Happily, I was invited to return on a part-time schedule. The department kept on the contract person to support in covering the massive territory I had previously covered, which made out for a manageable workload and minimal work travel. I reconnected with my colleagues, who I adore for their huge hearts and professional talents. I was reunited with a team full of wise, fun, supportive, and authentic people. Furthermore, I had actually been looking at taking a pay cut with the other department, and I ended up maintaining my level of pay and position with my home department. It was all quite magical, really.

It takes presence and curiosity to notice opportunities that are right in front of us, and sometimes a bit of courage and diligence to act on them. At times, what we really want is right there. At times, what we are busy searching for "out there", is right in front of us. At times, when it seems that other people have it better, what is best for us is actually right under our nose.

Shift Bit by Bit

When we continually commit to creating magic in small, inventive ways, the result can be a significant shift in our lives overall. We can find thrill, joy, and magic with a little courage and a few action steps. Perhaps you've already been moving in the direction of creating more and more magic, and want to shift even more. Perhaps you don't believe that a magical life is possible. Perhaps you just don't think you're cut out for magical adventure at all. Regardless of where you're at, I'm going to encourage and challenge you to create your magical life!

What if every day was a magical adventure in some way? What if you craved magical adventure? What if you sought magical adventure? What if you spotted magical adventure? A radical and magical shift in your life can happen bit by bit. Let's dig in.

Sometimes our view of what adventure is can be limiting. Adventure doesn't have to involve skydiving, or volunteering abroad, or buying a convertible, or trekking the Himalayas. It doesn't necessarily have to be risky, exotic, or expensive. From where we are right now, we can take on an adventure. For instance, what is something that you've always wanted to do in the place where you already live, but you haven't taken the time to do, or haven't had the courage to do?

Introduce magic into your life one day at a time. For instance, if you haven't been on a date night sans kids with your spouse for years, the first step is to go out once. The next step may be to make it a monthly commitment, and then perhaps a weekly commitment. If you haven't had sex with your spouse for months, the first step is to do it once...then again, and again. If your spouse has brought some ideas of sexual fantasies, but you've dismissed them, maybe it's time to give one a go. We can get caught up in bad habits and limited thinking that we think is okay. We justify our actions and thoughts, but really we are depriving ourselves of magic. One day moves to the next, and one month moves to the next, and before we know it, many moments of potential adventure and magic have passed.

Adding something into your life can create magic, and so can taking something away. It may be stress, a habit, negative energy, an activity, or a particular relationship that depletes you, and gets in the way of you creating and enjoying magic.

I don't like to admit it, but I used to fuss about what my kids looked like when we went out – that their hair was brushed, that their outfits matched (especially if they picked them), that they were wearing the "right" brand of clothing, shoes, and accessories. And honestly, I used to judge other peoples' kids for looking schleppish (yep, I made that word up).

But I've let go of this fussing because the energy it was requiring was limiting. The energy I was using to dress my kids and judge other kids wasn't all-consuming, but it did drain my energy. Letting go of worrying about and controlling how my kids look when we are out also freed me up to worry less about how I look in public. On my Friday mommy days, and many of my writing days, I sport yoga gear, sneakers, and no make-up. Or sometimes my make-up is a day old. I go out with dirty glasses and hair that hasn't been washed for a week or brushed that day; my legs (even wearing a skirt) aren't always shaved and sometimes I forget to wear deodorant. It is what it is. There is a tiny bit of magic that has been added to my life by letting go of that worrisome, controlling energy around appearances.

A few years ago, I decided to take a stand against having conflict and drama in my life. I've mediated conflict for over a decade – mainly workplace conflict, but also family, court, and community conflict. I'd learned a plethora of conflict management theories, models, and skills. And even though people in my life (usually family members) were eager to point out that my conflict management skills were far from perfect, I knew that I had advanced in my abilities to manage my emotions, listen intently, reflect others' feelings and perspectives, articulate my thoughts, and negotiate agreements. But the physical and emotional toll that being in the presence of conflict and drama took on me was far from magical.

I looked at my friends, and chose to spend more time with people who tend to be positive, who contribute to others, and who are focused on creating forward movement in their lives. I explicitly communicated to some people in my life that I'm not interested in conflict; if a fight arose, I reiterated that I didn't want to participate. If need be, I'd keep my distance. What was curious about this adventure was that there were people who were somewhat offended by my stand. Regardless of their reactions, I just kept saying that I was committed to light and supportive relationships. For me, being surrounded by powerful and passionate people is about as magical as it gets in life.

There can be a tendency in our society to think that a new job or a new house or a new relationship or a new city will create the magical shift we are looking for. But there is no silver bullet. There are so many aspects of life that we need to continually commit to enhance in order to keep bringing the magic. Shifting happens bit by bit, and with ongoing commitment, reflection, creativity, and action.

As like attracts like, magic attracts magic. The more moments and relationships and activities that we create that are magical, the more our lives will transform into one that is truly extraordinary in so many ways. It sounds magical, doesn't it?

Identify Your Views

Often, we have a few predominant ways of looking at life that influence how we see people, events, social situations, opportunities, etc. We have a mixture of perceptions about ourselves, other people in general, how the world works, and how life is. These perceptions color our thoughts, feelings, and decisions, and they point us down predestined paths.

Especially when these views are of a negative and dark color, they can significantly limit our ability to manifest magic in our lives. Our views can limit our ability to take on adventures. Our views can limit our ability to experience happiness and love. Our views can limit our ability to appreciate gifts from others and the universe.

Imagine that the sun is shining, the air is warm with a cool breeze blowing off the ocean, birds are chirping merrily, and someone pulls up beside you in a convertible covered in flowers, with the passenger seat open, and motions for you to hop in. You see a banner streaming from the backend that reads, "Come Along! FREE Adventure!" What if you were too busy looking at the sky wondering if it's going to rain to notice the attractive driver motioning to you? Or what if you did notice the car, and in your eyes saw a lonely person driving a ridiculous, hippy vehicle – a whacked-out fool, who has no friends, and who is probably looking to kidnap and assault a passenger. Either way, you are annoyed by the smell of the exhaust, the sound of the radio, and the vibrations of the motor. You curse under your breath and walk on.

It's important to become aware of how our views of life influence how we take action (or don't take action), how we react to situations, the goals we set for ourselves, and our relationships with others. The way we choose to behave, how we interpret what other people say and do, what we wish for and dream of, the depth of our connection to the people in our lives, is largely colored by the filters and views of life that we have adopted – often subconsciously. For many of us, we carry around multiple layers of filters that cover over each other. Opportunities for magic and positivity to seep into our lives are significantly limited by our filters.

Let's explore how our views of life can show up in common phrases and language. Below are some examples. I developed this list simply by listening to trends in what people talk about. I also looked at some of my own views that I have identified over time. By becoming more attuned to what other people say in their everyday language, and pondering how their views may be mirrored in their lives, we can also question whether similar views are playing out in our own lives.

I will caution you that you may start to feel annoyed, or discouraged reading these phrases, but stick with it. Sometimes we need to have the negativity of these views rock us to our core in order to truly recognize the impact they have on us. Start to pay attention to your internal dialogue, and the phrases you use. Which phrases can you find yourself relating to and using?

Life is Hard

- If it's not one thing, it's another

- Well, it was bound to happen at some point

- I'm getting by

- It just never ends

- I'm between a rock and a hard place

People are Stupid, Ignorant, Crazy, Weird

- They don't get it

- If only people didn't have their heads up their asses

- Those (insert ethnicity, profession, etc.) are such idiots

- She's not playing with a full deck

- She's a few bricks short of a full load

- He lives in a world of his own

- He's off his rocker

I Don't Need Anyone or I Can't Count on Anyone

- I'm a lone wolf

- It's lonely at the top

- I'm fine on my own

- I'll just take care of it myself

- If you want something done right...

I Don't Matter

- They'll just do what they want anyway
- I wasn't born special
- I've always been the neglected middle child
- They probably won't listen anyway

Something Bad Will Happen

- It's only a matter of time
- Don't count your chickens before they hatch
- It's going to hell in a hand basket
- Be careful what you wish for
- The light at the end of the tunnel is a train
- The shit hits the fan sooner or later

People Are Out to Get Each Other

- Watch your back
- Give an inch, and they'll take a mile
- People will only love you as much as they can use you
- I don't need anger management; I need people to stop pissing me off

Money is Scarce

- Money doesn't grow on trees
- It costs an arm and a leg

- What a rip-off
- A penny saved is a penny earned
- There's just never enough

The World is Wrong
- Well, it's typical...everything is messed up
- We are plagued by it
- It's still a man's world
- Fake people don't surprise me anymore; loyal people do

Men are Useless
- All they do is drink, smoke, and fart
- It's hard to find a good man these days
- I'm sick to death of men
- The useless skin around a penis is a man
- They're all lyin' cheatin' SOBs

I'm Just Putting My Time In
- Another day, another dollar
- The best part of my job is that my chair swivels
- We're just punching the clock
- 4,536 more days until I can retire
- Looks like it's f*** this shit o'clock
- Things I hate about work: humans and working

There's Never Enough Time

- I wish there were 50 hours in a day
- There's no time to explain
- To-do list: everything
- Sleep is overrated
- I don't have time for fun and games

Fight for What's Yours

- Drastic times call for drastic measures
- Keep fighting the fight
- F*** them all
- It isn't a crime to fight for what's mine

I Don't Matter

- They won't notice I'm gone anyway
- It's just little ol' me
- Hello, my name is "Easily Forgotten"
- You'll have more fun without me
- Don't worry about my feelings, because nobody else does

The Upper-Class Rule

- I'm still workin' for the man
- You need money to make money
- It's never fair

- You only win if you play dirty, and I won't play dirty
- The Republicans screw us; the Democrats pretend to care

I'm Different
- People don't "get" me
- If you were me, you'd know
- I'm not on drugs; I'm just weird
- I've always known I was special
- I pretend to be normal

Where do you hear yourself in these negative perspectives?

_____

_____

_____

_____

_____

What other views of life are you starting to see that you have?

_____

_____

_____

_____

_____

Whether you notice yourself or others using these phrases, I encourage you to start paying attention to the feelings that the words spur. Perhaps spend some time in a coffee shop or in the office lunch room or at a party, and pay attention to the types of conversations people are having. Begin to notice how their outlooks on life are feeding their experiences.

Although it probably won't be easy, persist in unveiling your own views. Simply by being open to reflect on our views, we can begin to identify them. To really dig into this self-awareness exploration, consider asking other people for feedback – or think about what feedback you've received over the years. If we ask other people what our flavor is, they may be able to identify it. This could even be a fun exercise and adventure to take on with a close friend. Be open to feedback. Keep in mind that the more open you are to what others say, even if it is hard to hear, the more you will be able to enhance your awareness and clear this subconscious junk.

See the Impact

These words that correlate to our life views roll off our tongues, often out of habit and unconsciously. They seem like casual words because it is such common language. We think it's just the way people talk, and just the way life is. We are blind to our own life views because they are ingrained in us.

We're not aware of how pervasive our views are. We even attract people and media that broadcast similar messages, so then we really think we have a valid outlook on life. We may choose professions, hobbies, social causes, etc. to participate in because the culture and norms and conversations of these groups uphold our outlook.

We speak these words, often without even realizing the negative energy that we create and perpetuate. The negativity — whether it is pessimism, judgment, helplessness, scepticism, or sarcasm — is embedded in the language and stimulates stress in the body, mind, and soul. There is little room for happiness and inspiration because we see darkness. There is little room for curiosity because we think we have life all figured out. There is little room for magic because we expect doom.

How do you see these views playing out in your life?

_____

_____

_____

_____

_____

What is the impact on you?

_____

_____

_____

_____

_____

What are you missing out on?

_____

_____

_____

_____

_____

How do your views impact your ability to create magic?

_____

_____

_____

_____

_____

It is worth considering where your views of life come from. Was it an experience as a child? Is this a view that runs within your family and/or a community of people that you spend time with? Perhaps a view adopted from media? Does your profession revolve around this outlook? Think about it, but don't worry if you can't figure it all out. More important than knowing where your views come from, is being aware of them and recognizing how they impact you and your life.

Our views of life are often hidden from us, and although it may be uncomfortable for us to confront them, it's worth it. By clearing the dirt, there is gold to be mined. Rather than being driven and controlled by a view that we don't even know is there, we can choose the outlook we want to take on in life with intention, so that we open ourselves up to magical possibilities.

Imagine a magical beach with crystal blue water lapping onto the white sand beach. The smell of fresh, salty ocean water is in the air. A local band is playing light festive music in the background, and a cold drink is sitting in the sand waiting to be drunk. You are sitting in a lounge chair wearing a hooded rain jacket in case it rains, you are sporting night vision goggles in case an apocalypse hits, you are holding a sword in one hand in case someone attacks you, and you are holding a sign in the other hand that says, "Don't Bug Me." You are committed to defending yourself against any threats and intrusions. You are blocking out the bliss surrounding you, and any potential adventure.

Happiness is around us all the time if we are open to noticing it, enjoying it, and amplifying it. No, life isn't perfect. Circumstances aren't perfect. But if we are always preparing for the worst, expecting something bad to happen, looking for what's wrong, and pushing people away, our chances of living a happy, inspired and adventurous life will be pretty slim. It's definitely worth looking at how our views may be restricting our potential to fully appreciate the magic of life from moment to moment.

Transform Your Outlook

Even just the awareness of your views and the conscious choice to take on new views can be enough to make a significant shift. Once you get present to the internal dialogue that runs you, and the negative impact that being run by this dialogue has on you, it is much easier to simply make a choice to see life and live life in a different way.

Chica 134

That said, a shift may not necessarily be easy because often our view of life is comfortable, like a favorite childhood blankey or stuffy. In a weird, comforting way, our view allows us to keep being a child and play small in life and pout, instead of trusting that life is inherently happy and inspiring. Interpreting, speaking, and behaving from an old outlook is habitual. Commitment to come from a new outlook requires the commitment to be someone different and do something different.

Taking on a new view puts us in the driver's seat of life, rather than in being at the behest of situations and other people. When we acknowledge that we have significant control over our own destiny, we can choose to enhance the extent to which we expect magic to happen, the extent to which we think people are good, and the extent to which we trust that we can flow with the events that occur in our lives. We can create our own success by believing in it, manifesting it, and celebrating it.

Imagine what each day would feel and look life if you took on a view that life is magical. We need to retrain ourselves to use new vocabulary. We need to retrain our internal dialogue. We need to retrain ourselves to have conversations with other people in a positive way. The outlooks and phrases below should help you to get a jump on this process.

One Step at a Time

- The journey of a thousand miles begins with a single step

- Keep walking the walk

- I may not be there yet, but I'm one step closer

- I don't have to see the whole staircase to take the first step

- One hour at a time, one minute at a time

The Past is Past

- I won't let the past steal my present

- Let it go

- I don't judge myself by the past because I don't live there

- What's done is done

- The past is an okay place to visit, but not a wise place to stay

- It's all over now

- I choose to forget the past; there's a reason it won't return

Life is Magical

- The possibilities are endless

- I am my only limit

- I always believe that something amazing is about to happen

- I'm too blessed to be stressed

- It's always my time

I am Powerful

- I've got this

- The harder I fall, the higher I bounce

- It may not be easy, but it'll be worth it

- Feeling defeated is only temporary

- I don't let my fear decide my fate

- I'm strong because I know my weaknesses

Success is a Choice

- I won't choose to fail
- Success doesn't happen by chance
- It will be what I make it
- I want to succeed as much as I want to breathe
- If I want a different result, I need to make different choices
- Giving up isn't an option

Mistakes are Okay

- I focus on improvement, not perfection
- Onward and upward
- I'm figuring out what works
- I don't cry over spilled milk
- I've learned what not to do, and that's valuable

Everything Happens for a Reason

- It's a blessing in disguise
- It'll unfold perfectly… maybe not as I planned, but perfectly
- It has been a good learning experience
- What if there is nothing wrong?

Work is Wonderful

- Do what you love and you'll never work a day in your life
- I love my job

- There is no distinction between my work and my play
- Life-fulfilling work is never about the money

People are Good

- Everywhere I look, people are offering to help one another
- She has a good head on her shoulders
- I'm grateful for how my friends contribute to my life
- He would give the shirt off his back
- We should cut him some slack

Obstacles are Minor

- C'est la vie
- It's not a big deal
- It's only a drop in the bucket
- I don't sweat the small stuff
- It's just a bump in the road
- Oh well, I'll carry on

Hard Work Pays Off

- There's a light at the end of the tunnel
- My hardest work leads to my biggest accomplishments
- Time and effort reliably produces results
- Those at the top of the mountain didn't fall there
- Hard work is like planting – it produces a harvest

I'm an Optimist

- I'm looking at it glass half full

- When it rains, I look for the rainbows

- I'm happy to be a Pollyanna

- It's a blessing in disguise

- If I turn my face to the sun, the shadows will fall behind me

- I'd rather look on the bright side

Life is Good

- It doesn't get any better than this

- Today I am thankful

- There's always a silver lining

- Life isn't perfect, but it has perfect moments

I Don't Fret

- I'll cross that bridge when I get there

- I'm taking it with a grain/pinch of salt

- No worries, mate

- I'll let it be

- I don't worry about what I can't change

- It is what it is

- I'll focus on what could go right, not what could go wrong

It Will Work Out

- The pieces will fall into place

- I'm just going to keep my chin up

- Time heals

- It'll work out for the best

- The sun will rise tomorrow

- Everything will be okay in the end; if it's not okay,

it's not the end

Money is a Blessing

- Money is energy; with high energy, I attract more money

- Generosity brings prosperity

- When I have money, I can contribute to worthy causes

- The more money I have, the more I can make a difference

- Abundance is a measure of the value I have contributed

I'm So Grateful

- I have an attitude of gratitude

- There are so many things to be grateful for

- I simply give thanks

- I don't take _____ for granted

- I trade my expectations for appreciation

After an exploration of limiting views, and a commitment to shift views, there's a much greater chance of seeing magic that's in front of you. Some people joke about, and warn against the perils of wearing rose-colored glasses. But there's a benefit to wearing rose-colored glasses. If you don't have them on, you could miss the magic, and actually not even know that you've missed it. In fact, there is value in wearing a number of different shades of rose-colored glasses, and being willing to try a few different shades on at any given moment, so that you are continually being open to, and seeking, the magic that's right in front of your eyes.

Practice, Practice

What was your reaction reading through the positive life views and associated phrases? Were you thinking that they are cheesy? Do these views seem foreign or over the top? Or maybe you already use this language and even have some of these positive quotes around you? There is no right or wrong, but your reaction in reading this piece may be a gauge for where you are at. I used to think that people who view life this way are fake... until I started hanging around more and more people with positive outlooks, and realized that not only are they authentically positive, but they are actually happy.

As you take on thinking, speaking, and writing (text, email, journaling, etc.) in these positive ways, really be conscious of the intention, meaning, and tone of your words. For instance, if you say, "I'm glad to be at the back of her" (meaning I'm happy when I no longer need to interact with her), there is a hint of gratitude in the statement, but at its root, there is a lack of respect and appreciation for the other person. There is also a lack of acknowledgment that even though you may have had challenging interactions, this person came into your life for a reason and a season – and brought learning. As we also explored in *Chill*, it's important to choose powerful words.

Start incorporating your new views into your conversations with people, and on social media. Rather than complaining about the state of a neighbor's yard, or judging another mother for something she does or doesn't do, or ratting out a colleague at work for an error, or sharing pictures of community crimes, focus on talking about how good things are unfolding in your life and all around you.

This isn't about pretending that life is perfect or that we are perfect. When people ask me how life is, I acknowledge the obstacles that I'm facing, while acknowledging that I am dealing with challenges powerfully, knowing that everything is unfolding for a reason. Here are some tips for speaking about the realities of life:

- Acknowledge the good – identify the blessing, especially in a messy situation.

- Acknowledge the bad – talk about challenges in a factual and non-dramatic way, rather than blaming self, others, or circumstances.

- Acknowledge your contribution – point to what you did (or didn't do) to create the situation.

- Acknowledge other perspectives – share different ways of looking at the situation so that you acknowledge what you are experiencing is not right, or the only point of view.

• Acknowledge learning – identify what you are learning about yourself and life, and how this learning will support your success going forward.

Because our reality is created from the views we hold and the language we use, I wanted to spend a substantial amount of time in this chapter exploring how our everyday thoughts and words – both the positive and negative – can color our world. When we are mired in the negative, our hearts and minds are swimming in negativity. When we practice focusing on the positive, we demonstrate to the universe our commitment to creating magic, and lo and behold, magic shows up. As renowned life coach Harrison Klein says, "Remember, to manifest means to invest attention in. Attention is your focused energy and it is sacred. Treat it as such."

Hang With Cool Cats

Imagine that you're at a magic show, and all you can hear is people all around you booing, farting, moaning, snoring, and yelling angry criticisms about how the room is too cold, how the magician is too old, and how the walls are full of mold. It doesn't matter how much you like magic or the tricks being performed, the experience isn't likely to seem magical.

If you have a choice to see the magic show at the theatre that smells like fart and mold, or the theatre infused with fresh oxygen and vanilla, which theatre would you choose? There's nothing inherently wrong or bad with wanting to enjoy the show in the latter venue.

"Cool cats" are people who enhance our experience of life – people who are positive, and people who lift us higher just because they do. It takes some conscious choosing to evaluate what cool means to you, and what kind of people inspire you. Ask yourself, "Does this person drain or fuel my energy?" If someone drains your energy, you don't need to explain why or how. If someone fuels your energy, prioritize spending time with her/him.

Growing up, through school, it often seemed to me that the "cool cats" were the kids who were good in sports, challenged the rules, wore nice clothes, got the trendy haircuts, dated five different people in a year, and had a nice house to hang out in. You probably weren't considered cool if you brought the school administrative assistant flowers. And you probably didn't earn the cool title for being the president of the "Students Against Drunk Drivers" club (that was me). As a kid, I didn't think that there was a lot of logic or merit in who was deemed cool, and doing what it took to be considered cool didn't always seem to be a good thing in my mind.

Later in life, people who are kind, creative, generous, savvy, and hard-working tend to be the ones who are truly successful, and who are the ones who are publicly recognized for their contributions and accomplishments. I think this is a good thing. We still have the option to be mesmerized by the pro-star athletes and pop culture drama. But from a girl who grew up in a small, rural town where some of the "cool cats" smoked, skipped school, partied, shoplifted, I'm sure relieved that it's a lot easier as an adult to find plenty of ambitious, warm-hearted, and compassionate people to hang out with – and to be proud to hang out with them. It seems to me that this is one of the true freedoms and privileges of being an adult.

Recently, on a vacation, my partner and I began talking with two young couples that we had met at a lounge in the hotel complex. They were explaining to us how the four of them had met, and how they were grieving because one of the couples was leaving the next day. With despair, one of the young women exclaimed to the other couple, "I can't believe you'll be gone tomorrow! We've had so much fun together! We have only known each other for two days, and yet I feel like we're so close, closer than our long-time friends at home."

This conversation instantly sparked my curiosity, and I began asking questions to explore why they thought this deep connection had emerged. The young woman said that she thought the four new friends had shared very openly with each other. She admitted that some of their friends at home seemed unmotivated and caught in habits and patterns, which includes using drugs frequently and watching a lot of TV. She said that friends at home talk all the time about "getting together", but that this is just an example of the superficial conversation and empty promises that float around because it never happens. She noted that she thinks people seem way more relaxed, happy, and authentic on vacation – there's less pretending, and less of a guard. She asked me, "So what would you say about this? How do you actually meet good friends in the real world when everyone is running around like crazy, absorbed in their own lives?"

It seems to me that the first critical piece is to assess your own mood and views. If it takes going on vacation to feel the magic, bring a smile to your face, and let down your guard, perhaps it's time to look at life at home and create a shift to bring more peace and happiness into your life – which will, in turn, attract some cool cats into your realm.

The next critical piece is to simply move from spending time with people who drain you, to spending time with people who fuel you, and to do so without creating drama. Notice when you hang out with people that don't support you in creating magic; notice the impact on your mood, ambition, and productivity. Then simply choose to spend less time with these people. This can be a gradual and gentle process for the most part. Some relationships may require more communication and diligence in creating distance and boundaries, so start with the relationships that you can ease out of.

You may be thinking, "Well, it's not kind or generous to just drop your friends all of a sudden." Imagine having a conversation with a current friend and saying, "You know what, I think we feed off of each other's negativity. We get in this cycle where we encourage each other to be judgmental of other people and we get stuck in accepting that our current life is as good as it gets. We complain about all of the crappy things that happen to us. But, I still want to be friends with you because I don't want to be mean by choosing to spend time with people who invigorate me." We can see how ridiculous the concern of growing apart from negative friends actually is once we lay it out on the table. Continuing to participate in relationships that perpetuate other people, and you, being stuck in life isn't doing anyone any favors or making you a hero.

Also, I'm not suggesting "dropping" your friends overnight. What I'm saying is that as you commit to creating more magic in your life, you are likely to bump into cool new cats synchronically. When you start to do something new, the circumstances and people around you are going to start to shift anyway. It will be a natural force that flows, rather than an action or process that you need to control or endure.

It is extremely powerful when you are creating magic to hang out with other people who are also committed to creating magic in their own lives and in the world. You are using magnetism of positive energy and multiplying your forces together. Our support networks are a key element to living a magical and inspiring life.

I think that one of the biggest mistakes we make is waiting for a ginormous swoop of magic that engulfs us – that, for instance, all of a sudden we would have the perfect friends and support network around us. Perhaps we think that a magical life would feel magical all the time, and our friends would all have utterly magical lives too. What's more realistic, I think, is to take initiative to continually infuse our lives with magic, including choosing the people we hang with.

Cheryl Bishop on...
Create Magic

"The human race is a very, very magical race. We have a magic power of witches and wizards. We're here on this earth to unravel the mystery of this planet. The planet is asking for it."

YOKO ONO

I interviewed Cheryl Bishop last year, and began writing her story shortly after our conversation, but I didn't complete the piece. A few months later, Cheryl checked in with me to see how my writing was going. I let her know that I was working on the book bit by bit, and that I still needed to finish writing her story. The truth was, I'd had some good weekends writing various chapters for *Chica* earlier that year, but at that time, my writing just wasn't flowing in the magical way that I often experience. I couldn't figure out what was blocking my flow. Cheryl was gentle and enthusiastic in her response, as she always is. She encouraged me to keep writing, and to stay in touch.

Finally, a few months later, it came to me. I realized that I was assuming *Chica* would follow in the footsteps of *Chill* – that I would highlight a number of women's stories in the final chapter of the book. But an inner voice told me, "That won't work this time. You need to incorporate their stories into the book." I was confused. I thought, "But the stories are too long to incorporate into the chapters. How am I going to do that?" One day I realized that each woman's story would be a chapter on its own, and that I needed to alternate one chapter of content with one chapter of story.

I contacted Cheryl to update her, to humbly acknowledge that I had been blocked in my writing, and to share that my inner voice had finally told me to make a shift in my approach in the book. Cheryl responded with genuine appreciation of the importance in listening to our inner voice. She emailed me back and said that she had to share with me what had just happened in her life. She wrote:

I went to Walmart to pick up some gloves for my boys, since the weather is getting very cold. I picked up two pairs of gloves and two toques. I was walking to the cashier and I could hear God say to me, 'Go and get three more pairs of gloves.' I could easily have ignored this message. However, I have learned throughout my life not to. So I listened and picked up $60 worth gloves and toques.

As I was driving home, I got the sense that I am to go to McDonald's, and see who needs gloves. I did not know what McDonald's to go to, so I decided to go to the one close to my home. I parked and looked through the window to see if anyone in the restaurant needed gloves. I noticed a person sitting there that looked homeless, but I saw that this person had gloves, so I left.

Then, heading toward home again, I thought that maybe I was supposed to go to the McDonald's at downtown Langley, which is a 10-minute drive past my home. I started to think, 'Aw, forget about it,' as I just wanted to go home and make dinner. Then I had to stay firm on what I thought I was to do, and I said to myself, 'Cheryl, it is only a 10-minute drive past home. If there is someone that needs the gloves you have, then you need to do it.' So I pushed myself to drive downtown.

I parked and looked around, but I didn't see anyone who needed gloves, so I asked, 'God, am I not hearing you correctly?' Ten seconds later, I saw a man who I have seen downtown before. He was almost running, as he always does, with two large plastic bags full of cans and bottles that he collects. I ran after him and caught up with him at the intersection at the lights. I said, 'Excuse me! Do you need gloves?' He turned, looked at me, and replied, 'Yes!' I gave him the gloves and said, 'Then these new gloves are for you.'

I walked back to my car feeling so thankful that I had listened to the message. My eyes started to water.

I went home and told my family that I had a God moment.

Then, after supper, my youngest son and I told my husband that we were going to the Dollar Store, which is right beside the first McDonald's I had been to earlier that night.

My husband said, 'I have a craving for McDonald's. Can you pick something up for me?' We said we would pick him up what he asked for, and off we went. When we got to the McDonald's, I noticed that the person I had first seen through the window was still there. This was an hour and a half later! She was walking out the door right in front of us. I commented to my son, 'She looks like she might be homeless.' My son said, 'Maybe she needs a set of gloves.' I went up to her and questioned, 'Do you need a pair of gloves?' She replied that she had a pair, so I said, 'These are new gloves. Do you know someone that needs a pair?' The woman responded, 'Yes, my son.'

I have many stories like this one.

~

Cheryl was born in Winnipeg, Manitoba, Canada. Her parents were living with their parents (her grandparents) on a dairy farm. At five years old, her dad decided that he wanted to buy the farm. They had almost signed the papers, but before they made the final decision to do so, they decided to take some time for a family trip to British Columbia. After exploring and relishing in the mountains and water of beautiful British Columbia, her dad called his father to say that they had decided not to come home and not to purchase the farm.

Her dad started pounding the pavement for work in Richmond. He became a realtor, a truck driver, and got involved in a few multi-level marketing companies, while Cheryl's mom went to school to become a hairdresser. Cheryl says she got her entrepreneurial mindset from her dad.

Cheryl's parents were very different, but they were in love — and still are. She says that her dad had a fifth grade education. He was the oldest of five children, so he helped raise all the other siblings. He had to get up in the morning and start milking the cows. Her mom is the oldest of three children and grew up on a lake with her brother and sister. Cheryl says, "It's amazing how two people can be so different, but so the same — and in love."

Growing up, she was shy. She says that she was always with her mom. She remembers the first day of kindergarten. She was devastated; she cried and just about ripped all her mom's clothes off because she didn't want her mom to go. "When you're familiar with something, you don't understand the world beyond what you're comfortable with," Cheryl recalls.

Cheryl explains that a defining moment in creating her mindset occurred when she was nine years old, sitting at the kitchen table, coloring. Her dad was writing a letter to tenants of one of their rental properties. Her dad said to her mom, "May, how do you spell car? Is it with an 'e' or no 'e'?" Cheryl says that as a young girl, she was told that she looked just like her mom, but acted and thought just like her dad. So, when she heard her dad ask how to spell car, she thought, "Wow, my dad isn't smart enough to know how to spell car! Wow, I'm just like my dad! Wow... I'm not smart enough!" This thought landed in her subconscious mind as a false belief.

It wasn't until Cheryl was 40 and in a seminar that she realized that this false belief had been planted in her subconscious programming for decades. She had gone through her life believing that she wasn't smart enough. Looking back, she began to see that she was a C (average) student and struggled to excel in school. She didn't feel that she was smart enough to even approach guys she was attracted to, let alone date them. And once she started working, she didn't think she was smart enough for the position that she had been hired for, or to even move up the corporate ladder. The subconscious programming had been holding her back in all areas of her life, and she didn't even know it. She was incredibly grateful to have discovered one of her blind spots in the seminar.

When she was in third grade, Cheryl's family moved from the Richmond bungalow to a bungalow in Surrey that grew to 4,500 square feet with her dad's handyman skills. The family lived there until she graduated. She began working full-time with the Royal Bank of Canada. Her colleagues kept encouraging her to develop her sales skills. "I was still really shy, but they assisted me to push myself out of my comfort zone."

In 1994, Cheryl and her soon-to-be-husband were about to get married. Her husband had lost his job, and they had just bought a house. Cheryl was determined to make a honeymoon happen for them. One night, after hosting a PartyLite home party, Cheryl asked the consultant how much money she had made that night. The consultant had said approximately $500. Cheryl thought that was good money for a couple of hours of work. She thought the consultant seemed a bit "flakey", and also found herself thinking, "Well, if she can do that, I can do that!" Cheryl always knew that she'd have a business, but she didn't know what it would be. PartyLite seemed like the perfect opportunity – she loved the product, loved that she could get out for some social and business time, and loved that she could earn the money they needed for their honeymoon.

She hosted a few home parties before Christmas that went great, and then in the new year, as she continued on this new adventure, she was really pushed out of her comfort zone. In April, she had six bookings for home parties and they all cancelled. "It's a sign. I'm not meant to do this," Cheryl thought. She called her leader – the "flakey" consultant who had put on Cheryl's home party. Her leader suggested that she call her past clients, go to their home and show them the catalogue, and ask if they wanted to book a party. Cheryl thought her leader's idea was crazy, and that it would never work. Despite her doubt, she got into action, and set out to prove her leader wrong. She knew that the plan was out of her comfort zone, so she would learn something regardless of the outcome.

Cheryl says that what fascinates her about our mindset is that we can think something isn't meant to be, and that we are receiving divine signs to quit, when really we are just tempted to cop out. She thought the party cancellations were a message that she wasn't meant to continue with PartyLite. But she booked a number of new parties by following her leader's advice. She ended up changing her perception, seeing that her leader was more wise and experienced than she was "flakey."

Chica 154

She thought she'd be with the Royal Bank forever, but in 1997, when their firstborn came into this world, she left the bank. She and her husband didn't think that her working full-time would work for their family. Though she had been with the bank for 16 years, she decided to focus on being with her children, and continue to build her PartyLite business.

She thought she'd be with PartyLite much longer, but in 2002, she started to lose her passion for the business. She had become a national Group Leader, and won a number of incentive trips. She loved the product, the part-time hours worked well for their family life, and she was making good money. The thought of leaving stirred guilt within Cheryl, because she had recruited a team of ladies who looked to her for leadership and support. She remembers, "God kept trying to tell me to leave, but my human mind didn't want to accept it." It took her six years to leave PartyLite.

After taking her kids to school one January morning in 2004, Cheryl came home and heard God speak to her, "I want you to go out your front porch, grab the newspaper, and read it."

She didn't like reading the news, because she found it too negative, but had learned over the years to listen. She found herself fighting back like a teenager, and thought, "Well fine! If I have to read the newspaper, I'm going to make a green tea and sit at the dining room table."

On the front page of the newspaper was an article about a woman starting a new pole dancing business. She was taking a pole into ladies' homes, to teach them pole dancing. Cheryl says this was before pole dancing was featured on Oprah, so it was still believed that only the "bad girls" were pole dancing. "Once anything is on Oprah, all of a sudden it's okay!" Cheryl comments cheekily.

She admired the leadership and courage of this business woman to embark on an adventure – to start a business focused on empowering women to boost their self-confidence, fitness, and sensuality. She picked up the phone to call the woman to wish her success.

The two ladies ended up having an hour and a half conversation about empowering women. This made Cheryl see more clearly how much she had a passion for empowering women; she saw that she had been doing this in her work at the bank, and with PartyLite.

Cheryl asked the business owner if she could check out a party, since she couldn't quite imagine what happened at these pole dancing parties. They were looking at dates on their calendars to find a time when Cheryl could join in on a party that a hostess was having, but the dates weren't working. Finally, Cheryl said, "You know what? We always go away for spring break, but we aren't this year. Why don't I host one?" They booked the party for March.

For the next three nights, Cheryl couldn't sleep, and during the day, all she could think about was that she needed to get involved in the pole dancing business. Cheryl says that it was as though God was knocking on her door.

She believed He was saying, "Cheryl, you need to get involved in this business." And Cheryl would respond, "No, no. This isn't for me. I'm a conservative girl."

She says that she kept thinking that she comes from a Christian family, and she didn't know how she would explain it to her dad.

She says that God kept knocking, and the third knock was so loud that she had to listen. So she called the business owner and said, "I cannot believe I'm saying this to you, but for some reason, you need to come over and talk to me about your business plan and the opportunity in this business."

The structure of the business was brand new, and Cheryl decided to purchase rights to a territory. The financial partner in the Pole Lot of Fun business was Colin Sprake. Cheryl and Colin became good friends through this business.

Cheryl says that she knew she was only supposed to do the Pole Lot of Fun business for two years. She ended up doing it for two and a half, so that she could support some training at the annual convention that Colin Sprake put on for the company. Colin ended up buying out the ladies that started the business. In 2007, Cheryl sold her portion of the pole dancing business. She and her husband had decided to move, because the area they were living in was changing drastically, and they didn't think it was safe for their kids. Cheryl decided to take a year off. She was going through some marriage challenges, so she wanted to take some time to work on her marriage, and look after her boys. She was sad to say goodbye to Colin, but the two of them had an intuitive sense that they would reconnect in the future. The following year, the economy went south in the U.S. and it knocked a number of the other owners who were still involved in the pole company sideways – including Colin. The money that had so quickly and easily flowed through the doors of head office, and each of the territorial businesses, was now flowing out.

Cheryl was standing in a Tim Horton's line up to get a coffee in the fall of 2008. She remembers thinking, "How could someone work for $10 per hour?" And then only a moment later, she got upset at herself. She scolded herself for being so judgmental of another human being and continued the conversation with herself. "How could you be so judgmental? Do you know their story?"

She made a decision that she needed to let go of her ego, teach herself a lesson, and get a job that paid $10 per hour. She was determined to learn and grow from this moment of realization.

She went home and opened up the online classifieds. She had time on her hands and decided to look for a part-time sales position. She had 10 to 15 hours per week to spare. She found an ad posted by a company that was looking for a mom with young kids to work 10 a.m. to 2 p.m. It paid $10 per hour. Cheryl went in for an interview. She says that it was a beautiful family that was running a sign company, and they informed her that she was overqualified. She shared what had happened in Tim Horton's, and that she wanted to work part-time for $10 per hour, and still maintain her time to focus on her family. The company accepted her, and within three months the position turned into full-time, because Cheryl was bringing in so many sales. It was time for Cheryl to depart, and for them to bring someone on full-time as Cheryl was not going to work full-time at this time in her life.

In January of 2009, Cheryl reconnected with Colin for a glass of wine. He had just started Make Your Mark, a training company focused on educating entrepreneurs in real-world business success. He asked, "Do you remember how we both sensed a few years ago that we were meant to do something together down the road?"

Colin said that he wanted to explore working together in Make Your Mark, but he needed to be completely up-front with her.

"I love and respect you, so I'm going to be completely honest. Right now, I can't afford to take anyone on. This is brand new. I'm starting from scratch. I don't have anything."

Cheryl asked Colin what he could afford so that she at least had something to consider. He said that he didn't want to disrespect her, but he could only pay $10 per hour. Cheryl looked at Colin and said, "Wow, I have a Tim Horton's story to share with you!" She accepted his offer.

Chica 158

Cheryl sees now how everything lined up perfectly. In 2005, Colin was going to start Make Your Mark, but the pole business opportunity had come up. Through the pole business, Cheryl and Colin met. There was tremendous value in Colin moving through the personal experience of a business failure, so that he could deliver the real-world business training that he dreamed of from a place of both empathy and experience.

Cheryl's biggest learning in life has been to always be open, and to always listen. She says that if she didn't pick up the paper on the front porch, and listen to herself in Tim Horton's, and listen to her intuition to get involved in the pole business (even when her mind was saying no), she would not be where she is today – side by side with Colin in Make Your Mark, supporting tens of thousands of entrepreneurs.

The other key to creating magic in life, according to Cheryl, is learning through communication. She says that when she was about 12, she saved up her babysitting money to buy a bathing suit. Proudly, she showed her mom the suit, and her mom said, "Well, that's just a piece of rag." Cheryl was heartbroken and devastated. She approached her dad, who was working in his office, and shared what had happened. She asked, "Dad, do you think this is a piece of rag?!" He said that the bathing suit looked nice and advised her, "Cheryl, everyone is so different. And for whatever reason, that's what your mom said. Maybe your mom has something going on. You should write her a letter to let her know how you feel." He suggested that Cheryl express her disappointment and hurt regarding her mom's comment.

She says that her dad is a brilliant man. He advised her to first and foremost avoid pointing fingers in the letter. He said, "Don't say, 'Mom, you make me mad.' Instead say, 'I was very proud that I took my own babysitting money and went shopping to buy something. And I thought it was conservative, not sleazy. When you said it was a piece of rag, my feelings were hurt."

What was revelatory was that Cheryl began to wonder about how her mom grew up, and how that may be influencing how her mom responded to situations, and interacted with her. She even began to wonder if maybe her mom was jealous – that she didn't have a good teenage life growing up. Cheryl said she started to wonder, "How can I communicate with her?" Cheryl says that the older she got, the more she kept reaching out to her mom, taking initiative to create connection. She says that eventually her and her mom could talk about anything together.

That commitment to learn through communication has created miracles in her marriage, as well. She says that everyone grows up differently, and everyone has their own perceptions. Two kids can grow up in the same family, but see things so differently.

One defining moment in her marriage was when she and her husband were at a New Year's party together. Cheryl was in the living room dancing with the other women by the TV, while the guys were hanging out in the kitchen and dining area. All of a sudden, a friend said that they were going to do the New Year countdown early, at 9 p.m., because they all had young children. Right away, they started counting down. Cheryl could see her husband about 15 feet away in the kitchen. Everyone was yelling the countdown... 10, 9, 8, 7, 6, 5, 4, 3, 2, 1. But her husband wasn't approaching her. She was looking at him and wondering why he wasn't coming to kiss her. She was making her way to him, and she says earlier in their marriage she would have gotten ticked off. But they were drinking and she didn't want to make a big deal. She went over and kissed him and wished him a happy new year.

She had learned over the years to moderate her emotions and not let events like this get to her. So two days later, she asked her husband, "I have a question. On New Year's Eve, I was looking at you while the countdown was on. I was wondering why you weren't coming to kiss me. How come you didn't?" He responded by saying, "Well, the woman should come to the man." Cheryl thought this was an absolutely fascinating perspective, because she saw it so clearly that the man should come to the woman. Cheryl says that was a defining moment and realization for her. She realized even though it was simple, really all of her and her husband's marriage problems were about how they each had a different perception of something. Cheryl's epiphany was how important it is to clarify and verify, when we react to anything. The key to success, she believes, is to always be working on our own mindset.

When she and her husband were going through that hard time, she would think, "What a jerk! What an asshole!" But she says what we think about, and focus on, expands. The more she thought that, the more her body language and words would reflect him being a jerk, which would cause a reaction in him, which would perpetuate their negative cycle.

A valuable lesson she has learned in self-control is to act as though you are role modelling to a child.

A perfect example of this was when one of her sons was 11 years old, and he wanted to sell some toys he did not play with anymore. He asked to have a garage sale. Cheryl said he could if he committed to be outside all day to look after the sale. Her son asked if he could invite his friend Cal over to help, and she agreed.

In the afternoon of the sale day, Cheryl decided she needed to go to the meat market to get some steaks for dinner. She noticed one of her son's bike leaning against her car, but as she was about to move it, her neighbor called her over. She talked to her neighbor for about 30 minutes and then jumped into her car.

As she started to back up and heard a loud crunching noise, she realized that she had forgotten to move the bike. She got out of her car to check out the situation, and said calmly, "Dang it."

Cal had been watching everything and asked, "Wow! Aren't you going to get mad?" Cheryl calmly responded, "Why would I get mad? It was my fault. I forgot the bike was there, and getting mad would not serve me in any way."

Cal said, "My dad would have cursed, kicked the tires, and hit the car." Cheryl commented, "Cal it is up to us how we choose to react to a situation." Cal had no idea that you don't have to get angry. That is why Cheryl is an advocate of acting as though you are setting an example to a child.

If we live our life like a little person is watching, then we become more aware of what we can do and can't do – or what we should do and shouldn't do. It's about acting with integrity.

At the end of the day, what keeps her lifted and drives her forward is her passion for making a positive difference with other people. She says it's important for all of us to be in touch with our raison d' être. In Make Your Mark, their mantra is, "When you focus on the money, you'll have dollars to count. When you focus on the people, you'll have countless dollars." Cheryl explains that this philosophy is the same as the biblical saying, "When you give, you receive."

She can see that one experience has led to the next with synchronicity in her life. Her dad's entrepreneurial spirit primed her to enter into direct sales. Her experience in home parties led her to entertain the idea of taking pole dancing. Her pole dancing business unveiled a friendship with Colin Sprake. Her Tim Horton's experience opened her up to take an entry level position with Make Your Mark. By listening to her intuition, even when she didn't want to, Cheryl found adventure, learning, happiness, and the next step on her path. Throughout her life she simply kept saying, "God, just allow me to hear you. How can I hear what I need to be doing?"

The point is to listen to intuition, divine messages, inner guidance, God's words, or whatever you want to call it. Over the years, she kept asking herself, "How can I hear what I need to be doing?"

She could have simply made choices without stopping to listen for the guidance. But she believes that she created happiness and success out of being open and listening. She began to recognize that the "loud voice" in her head was often worrying, being judgmental, putting herself down, and being negative. She needed to learn how to calm her "loud voice," in order to listen to the "quiet voice," which was optimistic and being a cheerleader. She says that it's a skill to tame the loud chatter in our own minds.

I can say that one of the most common questions and conversations that I have with people who are interested in working with me as a coach is, "How do I learn to listen to my inner voice?"

Cheryl's story illustrates what I believe. We need to trust in a higher power. We need to believe that we are deserving of extraordinary success. We need to learn how to recognize our inner voice. Cheryl says the phrase, "How can I make this happen?" has been a key one for her throughout her life. Rather than getting caught up with what other people say and think, and circumstances, she follows her intuition, one step at a time. In other words, both Cheryl and I truly believe that the ability to see divine messages, follow your intuition, and embrace magic is a learned, life skill.

www.karaderinger.com

www.peopleforpeople.ca

Annual People for People Conference
Edmonton, AB, Canada

Made in the USA
San Bernardino, CA
16 November 2019

59984173R00093